Contents

Introduction

Content Guidance

Questions and Answers

Personal Study

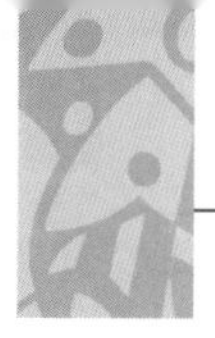

Introduction

About this guide

This unit guide is for students following the OCR AS Sociology course. It deals with the crucial area of **Applied Social Research Methods**, i.e. how sociologists find out about the society around them. Whether you are sitting the written paper (2537) or carrying out some sociological research/coursework in the form of the Personal Study (2538), this guide will give you the confidence to upgrade the knowledge and skills you already have in this area from your AS studies. A2 is designed to be of a higher level than AS, so you need to become more knowledgeable and skilful about the technical elements of sociological research. You will also need to demonstrate this higher level of methodological knowledge and skills in the synoptic assessment.

There are four sections to this guide:

- **Introduction** — this provides advice on how to use the guide, as well as an explanation of the knowledge required for these units and the skills you need in order to succeed in A2 Sociology. It also offers guidance on revision and advice on taking the unit test for students sitting the written paper (2537). For students following the coursework option (2538), the section offers advice on how to schedule your research effectively so that you do not run out of time, and an insight into how to score highly in the coursework assessment.
- **Content guidance** — this provides an outline of the essential knowledge required to succeed in the research methods units. Key methods, central concepts and many of the issues/problems associated with carrying out research are covered. Reference is made to evaluation points and useful writers.
- **Questions and answers (2537)** — this provides examples of the questions you are likely to face in the exam, along with candidate responses to the questions and examiner's comments on these responses. The examiner also points out how the marks are awarded and for what skills.
- **Personal study extracts and guidance (2538)** — for students doing the Coursework/Personal Study module, there is a detailed outline of what skills students need to demonstrate in each of the three major sections of the final report. In addition, there are extracts from coursework that are designed to show you what sort of detail to go into and what sort of language to use.

How to use the guide

To use this guide to your best advantage, you should refer regularly to the Introduction and Content Guidance sections from the time you begin to study Research Methods. However, if you are taking the written paper option (2537), we recommend that you do not attempt the questions in the Question and Answer section until you have covered most of the topic material in class and feel comfortable with it. When you

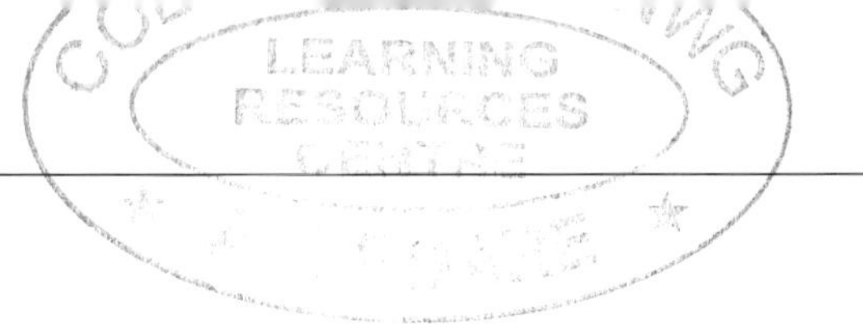

have reached this stage, take each question in turn, study it carefully and answer the different parts. Avoid looking at the candidate responses until you have completed your own. Try to write full answers, though you might prefer to start off by writing detailed plans for parts (d) and (e). (In the real exam you should *always* plan your answers for longer sections.) Consider the examiner's comments carefully — there are techniques to sitting exams, and you need to develop them. Learn from each candidate response. Look at the language used, ask yourself whether or not the candidate has demonstrated the skill(s) the question was asking for, and think of ways in which you might improve the response.

If you are taking the 2538 option — the Personal Study — you are advised to refer to the guidance about how to deal with each of the major sections of the report as you actually start to tackle each section. So, refer to the advice about the Rationale as soon as you begin work on your study. It won't do any harm to look at the guidance for the other two sections, but it is not necessary to study them in detail initially.

The A2 specification

The aims of the A2 Sociology course are to enable you to:

- acquire knowledge and a critical understanding of contemporary social processes and structures
- appreciate the significance of theoretical and conceptual issues in sociological debate
- understand sociological methodology and a range of research methods
- reflect on your own experience of the social world in which you live
- develop skills that enhance your ability to participate more effectively in adult life

In addition, studying A2 Sociology will ensure that you develop a deeper understanding of the connections between the nature of sociological thought, methods of sociological enquiry and substantive sociological topics.

Examinable skills

There are two examinable skills that you can gain marks for at A2. They are referred to as **Assessment Objectives** and you should note that you can only gain marks by fulfilling them. It is therefore crucial that you understand them, know how to demonstrate them and can spot where in the assessments they are being tested.

At A2, Assessment Objective 1 (AO1) is 'knowledge and understanding' and is worth 46% of the total marks. (It also includes the skills of presentation and communication.)

At first glance, this skill looks quite straightforward. In fact, it is not as simple as you might think. It is not just a matter of cramming as much content into your brain as

you can in those frantic days just before the exam! In order to demonstrate the skill of understanding as well, you will have to express your knowledge in a particular way. You cannot rely only on rote-learning, common sense or your personal opinions. Instead, you need to remember and refer to relevant sociological concepts, methods, theories and perspectives. Moreover, these references must be made in a way that shows that you understand, for example, how a particular concept fits into a key sociological debate.

In the units covered by this guide, you will need to demonstrate knowledge and understanding of:

- the ways sociologists gather primary and secondary data
- the ways sociologists analyse data and the concepts they use
- the factors that influence the research that sociologists carry out
- the ethical issues that arise in sociological research

In addition, you will need to be aware of the link between certain methodological approaches and particular perspectives in sociology. All of these issues are covered in the Content Guidance section of this guide.

Assessment Objective 2 (AO2) involves 'interpretation and analysis' and 'evaluation'. It is worth 54% of the overall mark for this unit and involves a range of skills. First, you will need to **identify** relevant facts, opinions, value-judgements, trends, etc. Second, you will need to be able to **analyse** data in various forms, and then **interpret** the findings in order to identify social patterns, trends, etc. Third, you will need to **evaluate** a range of factors, including the design of the investigation, the appropriateness of the method used and the performance of the researcher. Students often find it difficult to score well on evaluation, but essentially it involves making a balanced judgement about how well various aspects of a sociological study have been carried out.

Study skills and revision strategies (2537)

Study skills

From the very start of your A2 course it is important to understand that you need to be organised. This should not cause you any major problems if you follow the guidelines below:

- Keep your sociology folder in order. Make sure your folder has clear sub-sections, each of which should have a clear purpose. Date all of your work and write down the names of textbooks or other resources you have used.
- Regularly reprocess your notes — don't just leave them in original note form. Many students find that doing diagrams, mind-maps, charts, etc. helps to fix the ideas in their brain.
- Plan your week so that you work on sociology regularly. Set up a 'typical week' timetable on which you dedicate particular blocks of time to sociology reading,

homework and note-taking. Build in some sessions where you reprocess your notes.
- Make regular use of past papers. Get used to the structure of the paper. Practise writing answers in a timed situation.

Revision strategies

As you approach the revision period it is crucial that you find out and write down the dates and times of your exams. You also need to create a plan for the revision period on which you mark out the time you are going to dedicate to sociology revision. Then try very hard to stick to your schedule. Follow these guidelines:

- Devise a system of rewards that you can give yourself when you have done a good revision session. This could involve favourite foods, television programmes, leisure activities, etc. Whatever treat you choose as your reward, it should give you a brief break from your revision.
- Switch from topic to topic when you feel that you are getting a mental block.
- Create new sheets or cards on which you summarise essential knowledge. This could be a list of central concepts, or a diagram which pulls together the main research methods in sociology. Keep working on the knowledge.
- Make absolutely sure that you understand the format of the exam papers.

The unit test (2537)

Applied Sociological Research Skills is assessed by a 90-minute examination. Candidates are expected to answer one question which has five parts worth 60 marks in all. The successful candidate will demonstrate knowledge of key methods and concepts in research, the ability to analyse and interpret data, and the ability to evaluate different research methods and strategies.

The paper begins with **Item A**, which will be data relating to a particular research study or sociological problem. This could take the form of a piece of text, a table, a graph, a pie-chart or even combined text and statistical material which will give details of patterns, trends, findings, etc. It will also relate to and engage with methodological issues, i.e. issues about researching society. For example, it might contain a brief discussion about the virtues of a particular method. Item A will be followed by the question — parts (a), (b) and (c), worth 6, 8 and 10 marks respectively — which will link in some way with the content of Item A.

Part (a) will start with the phrase 'Using only Item A, identify *two*...'. This question tests your interpretation and analysis skills, i.e. how well you deal with the data accompanying the questions. It is therefore important that you take time to read and perhaps highlight the information in the item. The examiner may ask for two reasons, strengths, weaknesses, etc. related to the methods used by the research study mentioned in the item. The answer, therefore, is in the data, although you should not

be afraid to illustrate or to clarify what you have chosen from the item with your own knowledge. However, do not over-respond — this part is worth 6 marks only.

Part (b) will start with the phrase 'Identify and explain *two*' strengths, weaknesses, etc., which will relate to a particular method. This method may not be one mentioned in Item A but it is likely to be a variation on the same theme. This question tests your general knowledge and understanding of research methods. It is advisable to illustrate the two reasons, etc. with examples. Part (b) is only worth 8 marks, so do not spend too long on it. Two brief paragraphs should suffice.

Part (c) will start with the phrase 'Summarise what the findings in Item A tell us about...'. This part of the question tests your interpretation and analysis skills, so to do well you will need to draw out *all* of the significant findings from **Item A**, whether they are in statistical or textual form.

It is possible that the data in Item A could be in graphic form — in other words, in the form of a table, a graph, a pie-chart, etc. If this is the case, there is a simple but very effective set of steps to take when you attempt to extract the key points from the data. You will need to identify:

- the purpose/title of the data
- the source of the data (if possible)
- the year the research relates to
- the variables set against each other (in the case of a graph, these will be the things the axes represent)
- the units in which the variables are measured, i.e. the scale

You should be able to make sense of the information if you follow these steps. You will then be able to identify the following features in the data-piece, and you should draw them out in the following order:

- general/large or main patterns and trends
- specific/smaller or minor patterns and trends
- anomalies, i.e. things that stand out compared with most of the patterns and trends

Item B sets up a research situation for you to think about. This will take the form of an outline of a research proposal, i.e. you will be informed that an organisation wants some research done on a particular topic, and you have to imagine yourself in the role of the researcher and tell the examiner how you would carry the research out.

Item B will be worded according to the following framework:

> The (name of an organisation will be identified here) requires qualitative (or quantitative) data to discover whether (a particular hypothesis or research question will be identified here). You have been asked, as a sociological researcher, to design a proposal which will target a sample of (a particular research population will be identified here).

The remainder of the question comprises parts (d) and (e). In part (d), which is worth 14 marks, you will be asked to specify the approach you would adopt to study the issue in question. This part aims to test your knowledge and understanding of research methods and how they are applied through knowledge of sampling and operationalisation of the hypothesis and/or concepts associated with the research question. Six marks are available for knowledge and understanding of research methods and processes such as sampling and operationalisation. Eight marks are also available for evaluation. These marks can be picked up by justifying your choice of research method, sampling procedure and how you operationalise the research question in the context of the research problem identified in Item B. It is also important to remember that you will be rewarded for the accurate use throughout your response of the concepts of reliability, validity, representativeness and generalisability.

Part (d) will start with the phrase 'Outline and explain the research process you would adopt in collecting qualitative (or quantitative) data on (whatever the hypothesis/ research question is)'.

You should pay particular attention to the following in your answer:

- the practical reasons for your specific choice of method
- the theoretical reasons for your specific choice of method
- some discussion of the strengths of the method, though this should be linked specifically to the research context
- some discussion of how you might gain access to the sample population
- reference to a sampling frame
- reasonably detailed reference to the sampling technique most useful to the research context and why you have chosen it
- reference to how the research question/hypothesis and/or key concepts might be operationalised in the form of questionnaires, interview schedules and observation schedules
- if relevant, a consideration of ethical issues
- a brief reference to how data might be presented

Part (e), which is worth 22 marks, will ask you to evaluate the research idea you have put forward and offer possible solutions for any problems identified. It will therefore be worded: 'Assess the potential weaknesses of your research proposal, briefly explaining how you intend to overcome them'. Fourteen marks are available for knowledge and understanding of potential problems that you might face conducting research in a particular context. A further 8 marks are available for how well you evaluate your chosen research method, sampling technique, operationalisation, etc. in regard to the research situation Item B has put you in, and for the quality of the solutions you offer. As in part (d), you will be rewarded for the accurate use throughout your response of the concepts of **reliability**, **validity**, **representativeness** and **generalisability**.

You should pay particular attention to the following in your answer:

- potential practical problems resulting from your choice of method
- some discussion of possible theoretical objections to your choice of method, though these must be linked clearly to the research context

- potential problems with regard to how you accessed your research population, the use of your chosen sampling frame and the reliability of your chosen sampling technique. There should be some discussion of how these might impact upon the representativeness of your study and your ability to generalise from the likely results.
- potential problems resulting from your operationalisation of key concepts, e.g. social class
- if relevant, how ethical issues may impact upon the quality of your chosen research process and your findings
- some reference to how these problems might be resolved, e.g. by using triangulation or methodological pluralism, or by using a case-study approach. You must clearly justify these potential solutions by referring to their strengths. This discussion of potential solutions should make up a third of your response.

Candidates are advised to spend 30 minutes on parts (a)–(c), and 60 minutes on parts (d) and (e).

Scheduling the Personal Study (2538)

If you have opted to do the coursework option it is important that you manage your time effectively. Many students find themselves struggling to hit deadlines where coursework is involved. Following these guidelines will help to avoid this happening to you.

Getting started. It is important that you start thinking about your coursework at the very beginning of your A2 course. In particular, you need to decide upon a number of possible topics, one of which you will select as your final choice. You might find it useful to revisit a topic you found interesting at AS. Equally, there might have been a news story or event with a sociological angle that has caught your interest. (In this respect, it pays to keep in touch with the media. As you start your A2 studies, you should be reading serious newspapers and watching 'sociological' programmes on television.) Shortlist about three possible topics. Your teacher will help you to decide the final research question/hypothesis. You might need to scale down your ideas — students often try to do topics which are far too adventurous. A good way of finalising your choice — especially if you have almost got there, but not quite — is to try to link your issue to class, gender, ethnicity or age. After all, these are the aspects of social life which affect us all, and if your research question/hypothesis addresses one of them, it is more likely to hang together as a genuinely sociological project. Moreover, the research you do may be quite useful as evidence for the synoptic examination.

Work over the summer. You should make every effort to use some of your summer holiday to do two things. First, you need to do some research on the sociological method you are most likely to use in your study. Become an 'expert' on that method. Second, you need to read around your topic. There will be related studies on your topic, or something very similar.

Keeping a Research Diary. You need to record all the significant stages of your thinking and research relating to the Personal Study in the form of a diary. This should be on A4 sheets and should provide an insight for the examiner into what has gone well and what has not gone well over the time that you carry out your study. Make sure that you keep a (brief) record of all key developments, starting with the discussions you have with your teacher about the selection of your topic. Refer to any solutions you have found for any problems or challenges you have had to deal with. This information is important because it is likely to form the basis for the evaluation section of your Personal Study.

The proposal form. Once you have decided on your topic and research question/hypothesis your teacher will ask you to complete a form on which you need to tell the examiner a range of things about the study you hope to do. This form represents an important stage in the whole process, so you need to give it a lot of thought. You need to tell the examiner about the sample you intend to use, the method(s) you hope to use, the sort of issues you hope to explore, and any ethical or safety matters which might arise. You may need to give other details on this form — the key point is to make sure that the examiner is made aware of all your plans.

The timing of your primary research. Your teacher will give you guidance on this, but once your research device is finalised, you will be in a position to actually undertake your sociological research. Don't leave it too late. If you have to write letters to get your respondents lined up, start writing! In any case, the important point here is that you need to set aside a particular period of time in which you complete your primary work.

Internal deadlines. There are a number of internal deadlines, set by your teacher, to which you will need to pay particular attention. The most important ones are those relating to the completion of your research device (i.e. your questionnaire or interview schedule) and to the draft versions of the three major sections of the study — the Rationale, the Research section and the Evaluation section. Meeting these deadlines will lower your stress levels.

Unit assessment (2538)

You need to see the Personal Study as an exercise that allows you to be a sociologist, to research an issue you find interesting, and also to score highly in the exam. This is not an unrealistic way of looking at the A2 coursework option. In fact, the Personal Study is designed in a way that gives you every opportunity to demonstrate the skills that get you high marks.

The Personal Study should have three main sections — the Rationale, the Research or (Results) section and the Evaluation section.

The **Rationale** is the section in which you explain to the examiner what your topic is, why you have selected it, the method(s) you will be using, other sociological

studies your research links with, as well as a whole range of technical details about your study (e.g. the composition of your sample). The main skills you will gain marks for are knowledge and understanding. Be precise. Show a real understanding of how sociological research is done. Use appropriate concepts. You can also gain marks for analysis and identification by justifying the method you have selected. If you also state clearly why a different method almost became the one you selected, but you considered it to be less useful than your ultimate choice, you will gain evaluation marks too.

In the **Research** section, you will gain marks mainly for analysis and interpretation. This will involve how well you process the data or results you have gathered, how well designed your research device is, and how skilfully you have applied it. You could also gain knowledge and understanding marks in this section by using relevant concepts as you process your findings.

The final section is **Evaluation** and you should focus on making objective judgements about how well the study went, especially in regard to the research strategy (or approach) you adopted and the quality of the data you have gathered. There are other elements you can get evaluation marks for, and these are detailed in the final section of this guide.

Personal Study guidance (2538)

The Personal Study has to be a small-scale study, and one which focuses upon a clearly sociological issue. Your research question/hypothesis must reflect these features, and it must also be practical and not too ambitious. The central notion to grasp is that you need to carry out a manageable **pilot study** of the topic in question, not a full-scale study. What this means is that your key task is to design an effective, high-quality research device, then test it out (or pilot it) in a small-scale research activity which uses a small sample, and then evaluate the research activity. In this case, 'small is beautiful', so you do not need to administer a huge number of questionnaires, for example. Put another way, *process is more important than product* — students will not obtain higher grades by doing more and more questionnaires. In many respects, the quality, application and evaluation of the research device are the most important things. You also have to show the examiner that you understand the issues, such as ethics, which often loom large in sociological research.

In short, you need to:

- start with a clear research question or hypothesis
- devise a valid and realistic strategy
- carry out sensitive and thoughtful research
- analyse and interpret data systematically
- ensure there is a conclusion and evaluation of the research process and findings

Bear in mind the following key points:

- The coursework mark scheme is designed to reward a study based on **primary** research, although you could get some marks for a study which simply analyses **secondary** data. However, you should be aware that it is more difficult to get good marks for such studies, as they usually end up being little more than a summary of other studies on a particular topic. In other words, the student has not actually produced a research device — the very thing that can lead to high marks.
- Having made the above point, it is important to realise that secondary data *does* have a special role to play in the earlier stages of your work. Your wider reading will increase validity by giving you ideas about issues you might explore in your research. Reading about studies which link with your research will also give you ideas about how your research device might take shape. (If you can gain access to the original study you might find that it includes a copy of the research device used by the sociologist in question, and you might want to use some aspects of his/her research device.) You may be able to make brief references to related studies in your Rationale, and perhaps in other sections if appropriate.
- If you are aiming to score high marks, you have to become technically knowledgeable about doing sociological research. This means developing a detailed knowledge and understanding of the method(s) you employ, sampling issues, ways of analysing data, and a whole range of ethical and evaluative issues that arise when sociologists do their work.
- The overall word limit is 2,500 words. If you exceed this figure, the examiner will have to limit the number of marks you can obtain for knowledge and understanding, as some of the marks for this skill are for communication and presentation skills. If you go above the word limit, you will have demonstrated that you were unable to display knowledge and understanding in an appropriate and concise manner. Note also that OCR makes recommendations about the word count for each of the three major sections of the Personal Study.
- You need to make links with sociological theory wherever possible. Many students will be able to make a connection between their studies (and the strategy they adopted) and particular sociological perspectives. Concise comments about how interpretive approaches generally link with qualitative methods, for example, might be included. Equally, students might make valid points about the degree to which they managed to stay objective when carrying out their research. This is a form of theoretical point. Such comments are likely to be included in the Rationale and/or Evaluation sections. Whatever type of theoretical observation you make, though, ensure that it is expressed concisely. Equally, general theoretical points will not be rewarded — you need to ensure that your theoretical points relate directly to your study.
- You should keep a Research Diary as a means of recording significant points in your research experience. It can be used to record challenging situations and problems which might arise, as well as solutions adopted. These situations can be useful for gaining evaluation marks. If you make changes to your research strategy because of special circumstances, these should be recorded too. You could invite

the examiner to look at the diary by means of references to it in the main text of the Personal Study.

- When you process your findings you should use graphics (e.g. pie-charts, graphs) only if they represent the best possible way of presenting your data. Students often feel obliged to put data into graphic form because it looks attractive. On many occasions, though, well-chosen quotes from your respondents can be the best way of presenting data.
- The quality of your research device is highly important. You will gain more marks if you construct and apply a research device which has a sound structure, which operationalises the central concepts involved, and which is on an appropriate scale.
- You should choose a topic which meets certain criteria. First of all, it must be a topic which interests you — this unit will take up a fair amount of your time, so choose something that you won't get bored with. Next, choose a topic which links up with a subject you are studying in another unit (e.g. crime or education). That way you will develop a detailed knowledge of the area in question. (It is possible to choose a topic which is not on the specification, and many of these studies are done well. However, this is a slightly more risky approach to adopt.) Finally, remember that you would be wise to build into your study one of the key dimensions of the synoptic unit. In other words, try to build social class or gender or ethnicity into your study. If you do this you will stand a good chance of benefiting in the synoptic unit exam, as your knowledge of inequality and difference, and also of researching these aspects of social life, will be much greater.

The Rationale section

The word rationale means 'an explanation of your reasons', so this section has the key role of allowing you to tell the examiner many important points about your study. **At the start of the Rationale** you need to state your research question (or hypothesis or research focus) very clearly. Once you have done this, you need to do the following:

- Break the research question down into sub-questions (perhaps three or four). These will be your aims, and you can put them straight after the research question. Introduce them with the statement: 'My aims are to answer the following questions:...'. These aims are central to a successful Personal Study, and once you have established them, you can refer to them at key stages of your work.
- State your objectives. These are best understood as the practical tasks you need to carry out in order to pursue your aims. A typical objective might be: 'To conduct a questionnaire survey of 15 respondents'. A good study normally has three or four objectives.
- Tell the examiner what your research strategy is to be. This means stating the main method you intend to use (plus a supporting method if appropriate), plus the essential details of where and when your primary research will be carried out. Don't leave the examiner guessing — write down all the basic details.

- If you are going to use questionnaires, don't just state the fact and leave it at that. There are different types of questionnaire — the examiner will want you to be specific about the particular kind you are using. Is it a direct questionnaire or a postal questionnaire? Whichever you are using, give as much detail as you can.
- Tell the examiner why you have chosen your research question. Did you select it because it has been prominent in the media recently? Or is it a topic which caught your interest in class? Whatever the reason, you need to show the examiner that there is a good sociological basis for your choice.
- As mentioned earlier, the examiner will want to know as much about your research strategy as possible. In particular, you need to justify your method, and you must do so by showing why the method selected is the most appropriate one for your particular study. Don't just make general observations about questionnaires and their strengths. You might also state the method you almost selected, but finally rejected, and why. When you tell the examiner about the strategy you plan to adopt, you should use the key concepts in research methods as much as possible. These, of course, are reliability, validity, representativeness and generalisability. When justifying the method you have selected, you will mainly be referring to validity or reliability.
- Tell the examiner about the sample you will be using. A number of points are important here. In particular, the examiner needs to know about sample size and sample composition (i.e. the ethnic and age composition/proportions of your sample). You also need to say which sampling technique was employed, e.g. quota sampling or snowball sampling. It is clear that sampling decisions made by researchers have very real consequences for representativeness and generalisability.
- Regarding your strategy and sample, you should tell the examiner about any issues relating to access that might have arisen. If you researched a sensitive topic, e.g. bullying in school, you might have found problems gaining access to a sample of victims.
- Make a brief reference to a secondary study that links with your study. Be careful not to get carried away — the word limit will not permit you to give too much detail. However, studies which have inspired you or that you want to replicate do need to be mentioned.
- Make some reference to the 'theoretical base' of your study. In particular, if you are researching gender issues, it is possible that you might wish to link your work with the feminist perspective in sociology. Equally, if you are adopting a largely qualitative approach in your research, it might be appropriate to make some reference to the interpretive tradition in the discipline. Make sure that you provide appropriate references for any studies you mention in this section. (This also applies to other sections of the Personal Study.)

The Research section

In this section you need to present your findings, analyse and interpret them, and draw some conclusions. As you process your findings in this section, you should keep

referring to the aims you established in the Rationale. A good Research section will take account of the following points:

- Describe your research device briefly, and make a special point of stating how you have operationalised the concepts which are central to your study. You should also show that you understand clearly that your key task is to pilot the research device.
- Remember that the examiner is looking to see you apply a high-quality research device, so make it clear that you have spent a lot of time and thought in designing your device.
- Indicate whether any special circumstances or issues, e.g. ethical or access issues, have played a part in the way you have carried out your research.
- Give a clear heading for the results you present, e.g. 'Questionnaire survey results'.
- Analyse and interpret your findings item by item. Don't use graphics unless they are really necessary. As you work through your data, you should tell the examiner what the findings for each aspect of the research device are, and then state their significance with regard to your research question and aims. For example, if you use a questionnaire, you should work through each item's findings and say how each aspect of the data gathered gets you closer to being able to answer your research question because it links with one of your aims. Key trends and patterns should be identified, or revealing quotes stated clearly. What you need to do, in fact, is provide a commentary for the examiner. Remember the phrase 'the evidence does not speak for itself' — you need to speak for it.
- If you are doing content analysis, or observation, or any primary method, you have to go through this process systematically. Take the data you have gathered and draw out their significance for the examiner.
- At certain points, especially when you have presented an element of the data which you may see as particularly important, you might want to draw an interim conclusion. This is a speculative conclusion, which you draw when only a part of the data has been analysed, but which you think is justified, given the way the evidence is pointing.
- If you have referred to a key related study in your Rationale, you may be able to make some brief comparisons between the findings in that study and the ones your study has generated.
- As you process your findings, ensure that you do not 'drift' from your stated aims. If you keep looking at your research question and your aims, you will stay on track, and your analysis and interpretation of your findings will remain relevant.
- Finally, draw your conclusions. It can be useful to say, first of all, what the data tell you in terms of your aims. You can then finish off with an overall conclusion — which will, of course, correspond directly to your research question (or hypothesis). However, you might decide that your findings do not allow you to draw a final conclusion. In that case you should make cautious statements about what your research suggests, or what indications it gives. This is not a problem. Provided that you have carried out the research effectively and analysed and interpreted the data properly, there is nothing wrong with presenting tentative indications rather than a firm conclusion.

The Evaluation section

In the final section of your Personal Study you are asked to look back over the whole exercise and review it. You need to give a balanced judgement about what went well and what did not (and why). In many respects, this section and the skill of evaluation itself involves asking yourself a series of 'awkward questions' about how well the Personal Study went. However, this need not be painful, because you can gain marks by pointing out weaker aspects of your study (as well as, of course, the stronger aspects). It is vital that you carry out this exercise using the central concepts of sociological research — reliability, validity, representativeness and generalisability — so make sure that you apply them appropriately in this section. Ask yourself the following questions:

- **Were the research question (or hypothesis) and the aims I used clearly sociological and properly focused?** As you look back to the very earliest stages of your Personal Study you will remember the time you spent refining your title, and the question you need to ask yourself is: 'Did I succeed in producing a title which was appropriate for my purposes?' Did it allow you to research the 'angles' you wanted to examine, was it on the right scale for a pilot study, and was it realistic? (Your aims should be subjected to a similar scrutiny.) These are the key things to consider in this respect, though you might identify *other* aspects of the research question that need to be evaluated.
- **Did I select the most valid method for my study?** This is clearly a crucial question. In retrospect, was the method you opted for really the best one for the job? Did it deliver the data you wanted? In all honesty, do you now feel that an alternative method might have worked better?
- **Was the overall strategy I adopted appropriate?** If you used more than one method, ask yourself whether they complemented each other. Was the sample appropriate? Was your general way of organising the research process effective? If not, consider how it could have been improved.
- **Was my research device of a high quality?** You could consider the device as a whole, e.g. asking questions about the number of items you had on your questionnaire, if you used that method. Equally, you could consider the effectiveness of particular items on your questionnaire — which worked best and why.
- **Can I draw conclusions effectively from the data gathered?** There might be gaps in the data which you now see could have been 'plugged' if you had, say, used a different method, or asked different questions in your interviews.
- **How did I perform as a student sociologist?** Consider whether you were able to maintain a fair degree of objectivity when you carried out your interviews. Analyse your organisational skills, and consider whether your conduct was always ethical.
- **How might this study be improved, or developed further?** If you used one method only, would some form of triangulation or methodological pluralism have improved the general effectiveness of the study? If you examined gender issues in your research, do you now feel that social-class dimensions should have been explored too?

Ask your teacher for a copy of the mark scheme for the Personal Study. This will confirm to you that the above guidelines for the three key sections will actually help you to gain high marks if you follow them carefully.

In addition to the main three sections, your Personal Study needs to have a range of other, smaller components. The complete list is:

- **Title page**
- **Contents page**
- **Rationale**
- **Research**
- **Evaluation**
- **Bibliography and resources** — this is a list of all the resources you have used in your study. Clear referencing is important.
- **Appendix** — this should include a copy of the approved proposal form, plus a clean copy and a completed copy of the research device used. Any letters written in connection with the research should also be included.
- **Research Diary** — this should be presented on sheets of A4 paper.
- **Annexe** — all the raw data you gather should be kept safe by you or your school or college. It should not be sent to the exam board unless specifically requested.

Content Guidance

When sociologists study social behaviour they tend to either ask questions or observe. There are other ways of examining society, but variations on these two approaches tend to dominate. This section is designed to familiarise you with vital knowledge about **research methods**. You need to know, understand and evaluate:

- **the full range of research methods (both primary and secondary)**
- **a number of key concepts related to sociological enquiry**
- **the particular problems and issues that arise in sociological research**

The content in this section is offered as guidance only — it is not exhaustive and there will certainly be other concepts and studies that are useful in addition to those we mention. With regard to your studies, whatever textbook you use will contain sufficient examples for your needs, and your teacher will undoubtedly refer you to others. If you have back copies of *Sociology Review* in your library, you will also find a number of useful articles on this area of the course. In addition to 'studies', i.e. pieces of sociological research, there are many books and articles in which sociologists discuss their ideas about an aspect of methodology. These will be referred to in your textbooks.

The OCR A2 topic of Applied Sociological Research Methods intends to develop a good understanding of the practical, technical and theoretical aspects of 'doing sociology'. To achieve this, you will need to study methods, concepts, problems and issues, as outlined above. It will also be advantageous to learn the strengths and weaknesses of each method. Furthermore, it is advisable to build up your knowledge of a set of central studies linked to the key methods. These can act as examples that you can use to demonstrate to the examiner a good understanding of sociological methods.

Research design and sociological theory

Essential concepts in sociological enquiry

This section gives you a list of concepts which will help you understand and explain what sociologists do when they attempt to make sense of the social world. A concept is an idea which helps us make sense of our experiences, so in the context of sociological research, they relate to aspects of using both primary and secondary methods. In terms of exam success, they are crucial — they allow you to show a high level of knowledge and understanding, and help you to address complex issues in a concise manner.

Reliability

This concept relates mainly to the process of carrying out sociological research, and is concerned with the way in which data are gathered.

- The issue of reliability asks questions about whether the evidence-gathering process is scientific. Some sociologists argue that 'replication' is an important characteristic of scientific method, i.e. if another sociologist is able to repeat (or replicate) your study using your method and a comparable sample, reliability is said to be high if the same (or very similar) findings were obtained. It would also show that all other factors which might affect the results had been controlled.
- At a basic level, researchers can guarantee reliability by, for example, ensuring that the items on the questionnaire they use are all standardised, i.e. that every respondent looks at identical items.

Validity

This means the degree to which the research activity actually measures what it sets out to measure.

- Imagine that you want to study the effects of screen violence on young people. You might be inclined to carry out an interview survey in order to find out their experiences of watching violent films and whether or not they believed that this had made them more violent. However, this strategy and method would *not* be valid. What you would actually be doing is gathering data about young people's perceptions of whether they had been negatively affected by media content, rather than the effect of screen violence on young people. You would certainly have gathered related data, but you would have 'drifted' from your original research aim. Validity is about selecting the method which will 'deliver the goods', i.e. the specific data you want, and not just related data.

- Validity is also about the degree to which the sociologist has been able to operationalise (see below) the central concepts, aims and issues in the study. If this has been done, the research device will measure what it sets out to measure. For example, if you were studying the domestic division of labour and wanted to see if roles between male and female partners in households were generally equal, you would have to build into your research device elements which would allow you to test out this matter in a thorough and imaginative manner. Otherwise, you would miss many aspects of family life which might reflect equality, and your research device would lose validity, as would the whole study.
- The term 'validity' is often used when sociologists consider, for example, the value of the 'end result' of sociological research. For example, the product of data-gathering activities on crime, i.e. the official criminal statistics, is often criticised for not being a true measure of the amount of crime in society.

Representativeness

This concept concerns sampling. It is possible to see a representative sample as a 'scaled-down version' of the whole population which has the same social features as the whole group. For practical and cost reasons it is often impossible to survey or study whole populations, so sociologists construct samples which 'represent' the larger population, i.e. they have the same characteristics as the whole population and in the same proportions. For example, the ratio of males to females in the sample will reflect that in the whole population, as will the proportions of different ethnic groups, different age-groups, and so on. People in the sample are typical of people in the wider society. The notion of representativeness has clear links with the concept of 'generalisability'.

Generalisability

The idea of generalisability means that the researcher takes the findings or conclusions from his or her sample study and makes the assumption that they can be applied to the whole society or larger social groups to which the sample belongs. This can only be done with confidence if the sociologist has used a representative sample. So, for example, at the time of a general election, when researchers say that their surveying suggests that the vote is going to go in favour of a particular political party, we should be wary of their statements unless we are sure that they have asked a representative sample of potential voters how they intend to vote. It is unlikely that any other form of sampling will be an appropriate basis for generalisation.

Choosing research methods and devices

Theoretical constraints

Sociology textbooks on methods have traditionally suggested that when it comes to choosing a research device, sociologists have generally fallen into one of two theoretical camps: positivism or interpretivism. Whether you are responding to parts (d) and (e) of the 2537 examination or constructing a Personal Study, it is important to understand that few sociologists today are straitjacketed by these theoretical labels. Rather, good empirical sociologists choose whatever methods work best and this may involve a combination of methods traditionally associated with either the positivist or the interpretivist position. However, it is a good idea to have some knowledge and understanding of the principles that underlie each theoretical position because these may form part of the rationale for your own choice of method and the design of your research device.

Positivism

Just as natural scientists believe that behaviour in the natural world of animals, plants, chemicals, etc. is the product of natural laws, positivist sociologists believe that human behaviour is the product of 'social laws' which arise out of the way societies are socially organised.

Positivist thinkers believe that sociology is a science and should adopt four principles that underpin the logic and methods of natural sciences such as physics and chemistry:

(1) Research should be carried out under controlled conditions, such as experiments in laboratories. However, sociologists rarely use laboratory experiments. Instead, sociologists stress that control should be achieved through sampling and skilfully-designed questionnaires and interview schedules.

(2) Research should be objective or 'value free'. The sociologist should carry out research and interpret all evidence with an open mind, setting aside personal or political beliefs and prejudices. Personal views and values may distort the research and result in unreliable and invalid findings.

(3) Research should be designed in such a way that other sociologists would be able to inspect the research device, replicate it and obtain similar results in order to verify the evidence gathered and check the reliability of the research device.

(4) The research method should be designed so that it generates mainly quantitative data, i.e. statistics that can be converted into tabular or graphical information. Such data have comparative value because they can be observed for patterns, trends, etc. and for cause and effect relationships in order to establish 'social facts' or laws about human behaviour.

Positivist methodology in sociological research has tended to focus on the use of quantitative methods, such as the social survey which incorporates questionnaires and structured interviews. Although the survey is the main tool of positivist research, positivists have also used experiments, the comparative method, official statistics and content analysis of mass-media reports. Such methods tend to be used by macro-sociology, i.e. research that investigates large-scale social processes, structures and institutions such as the social class or educational system.

Key concepts

reliability; validity; representativeness; generalisability; positivism; social laws; science; objectivity; value freedom; quantitative; macro-sociology

Interpretivist sociology

Interpretivism, which is sometimes referred to as 'anti-positivism', action theory or phenomenology, rejects the positivist idea of determinism, i.e. that social laws shape human behaviour. Interpretivist sociologists suggest that society is the net product of individuals interacting with each other in social groups. Moreover, we bring a set of shared meanings or interpretations to these interactions which help us make sense of our world. We all know how to behave in most situations, e.g. at a funeral, because we have learned these shared meanings. Interpretivists therefore argue that sociological research should focus on the meanings that people use to make sense of the social world.

When it comes to choosing a research method, interpretivist sociologists stress the following factors:

- The interpretivist sociologist believes it is important to appreciate how the world looks from the point of view of those being studied, to see how they interpret the world and why their interpretations take a particular form. This is a form of empathy called *verstehen*.
- Validity is emphasised. Interpretivists believe that unique and trusting relationships should be established with those being studied so that a true picture of their lives can be constructed, although some sociologists suggest that a by-product of this is that reliability is sacrificed.
- Cause and effect relationships are thought to be impossible to establish in regard to human behaviour because such behaviour is unpredictable. The meanings or interpretations people attach to their everyday experiences often change.

Interpretivist methodology in sociological research has tended to recommend the use of qualitative methods such as unstructured interviews and observation. Interpretivist sociologists have also used methods such as historical and personal documents as well as semiotic analysis of mass-media reports. Such methods tend to be used by micro-sociology, i.e. research that investigates everyday interaction, especially face-to-face behaviour such as that which may occur between doctors and their patients.

Mixing theoretical approaches

You need to know and understand the above theoretical perspectives in sociology and why each favours particular methods. However, the idea of mixing methods from different theoretical traditions is not a new one. Researchers often use both quantitative/positivist and qualitative/interpretivist methods. For example, Phizacklea and Wolkowitz (*Homeworking Women*, 1995) use both a national survey and in-depth interviewing to increase validity.

What you need to realise is that the examiner is looking for *contextualised* knowledge and links relating to theory and methods. She or he will not be able to give high marks for generalised comments in the 2537 exam or in the Personal Study about theory and methods. Many candidates fail to pick up marks in parts (d) and (e) of the 2537 examination because they are too concerned with describing elements of positivist and interpretivist theory without making clear how it relates to the research context of the question. This contextualisation is essential if you are to get high marks. Equally, if you are doing the Personal Study, any comments you make about theory and methods *must* relate clearly to the sociological issue you are researching.

Finally, it is worth noting that while theory has a role in deciding what the most valid method for a particular study should be, it is rarely the sole determinant of the method selected. Practical, ethical and cost factors could all play significant roles in the final choice.

Key concepts

interpretivism; social action theory; anti-positivism; phenomenology; shared meanings/interpretations; interaction; qualitative; *verstehen*; micro-sociology

Practical constraints

Cost and funding

The cost of the research is a crucial factor in determining the topic of research, the hypothesis and the method to be adopted. If the sociologist does not have access to large funds, cheap methods will be required. These might include any of the following:

- A questionnaire survey only involves paper printing and postage costs and may therefore be preferable to the expense of hiring interviewers who need to be paid.
- Group or focus interviews might be chosen because they are a cheaper alternative to carrying out a series of individual interviews.
- The longitudinal nature of many observation studies means that some sort of financial support is required, perhaps over a period of years.
- Some types of data are already cheap, e.g. secondary data that has already been collected.
- If funds are available, researchers may be able to adopt methods which are more ethnographic and longitudinal, e.g. observation studies.

Candidates for Unit 2537 should note that their choice of method for parts (d) and (e) is not dependent on cost or funding. You can assume that these are covered by the organisation sponsoring your research in Item B.

Access

Gaining access to a group of respondents that you wish to interview or administer questionnaires to, or getting into a group you wish to do ethnographic research with, can sometimes be very difficult. Sociologists need to ask themselves four essential questions, i.e. whether the research population is:

(1) accessible
(2) deviant and therefore potentially threatened by the research
(3) literate or illiterate
(4) geographically scattered across the country or concentrated in one place

Difficulty of access to a sample might mean that a preferred method (in-depth interviewing, for example) would have to be changed (perhaps to questionnaires). This is not uncommon when the issue is a sensitive one, such as deviant sexual behaviour or mental illness. Joining 'exclusive groups' which tend to shut out 'outsiders' or gaining access to them to conduct questionnaires and interviews is not impossible but needs to be thought through carefully in terms of both ethics and personal safety.

Very often, the sociologist will need to use an intermediary or 'gatekeeper' — a person who has contact with a relevant or appropriate set of individuals. For example, access to victims of domestic violence is not easy. An intermediary plays a key role, since she or he can perhaps vouch for the researcher and help establish a bond of trust between the sociologist and the group in question. Key professionals can sometimes fill this role. For example, social workers can often introduce a researcher to women who have been abused. Such intermediaries are particularly useful for introducing participant observers into a group and reducing the anxieties of other group members who may feel threatened by the newcomer.

Sampling

This concept relates to the process by which sociologists select research subjects from a list known as a **sampling frame**. Note the following points about sampling and sample frames:

- The sampling frame must have the general characteristics required for the study in question. For example, it must be a population of teenage mobile-phone users if the study is looking at young people's usage of mobiles in public places.
- The sampling frame has to be up-to-date. If you were studying doctors' strategies for dealing with stress at work, you would want a sampling frame which had on it the names of doctors currently practising, not one that also included names of doctors who had retired.
- The electoral register is the most common sampling frame used by sociologists but it excludes certain groups, i.e. those aged 17 and under, prisoners, those

avoiding paying council tax. Moreover, if it is used months after it is compiled, it will include people who have died or moved away and will not include those who have recently turned 18.
- The Postcode Address File is increasingly popular as a sampling frame.
- Other examples of sampling frames include school registers and doctor's registers. However, permission to use these may only be granted if you can guarantee anonymity, confidentiality and ethical sensitivity, and demonstrate that your research will have positive benefits to the community.
- Deviant or unconventional groups are rarely represented by sampling frames.
- Maps are sometimes used as sampling frames in the absence of lists of particular types of individuals. Sociologists may select areas on a map randomly, then streets within those areas, and target all households within them.

Samples can be described as random samples or non-random samples. With the former, everybody in a given population has an equal probability of being selected for the sample. Sociologists prefer to use random sampling methods in order to minimise the possibility of bias. It is believed that some types of random sampling are most likely to result in representative samples, i.e. those which in terms of their social characteristics most resemble the population being studied. Representative samples are thought to be important because they allow for the possibility of generalising any data collected to the general population under scrutiny. There are various types of **random sample**:

- **Simple random sampling** involves selecting names from a sampling frame at random. This could be done with a computer. The lottery (Lotto) is a good example of this type of sampling. However, this method of sampling does not always guarantee a representative sample.
- Sociological research tends to use **systematic sampling**, which involves choosing every nth person from a sampling frame. For example, 10 people out of a group of 100 may be chosen by randomly selecting a number between 1 and 10, e.g. 8. Every tenth name after 8 is selected, i.e. the sample consists of numbers 8, 18, 28, 38, 48, 58, 68, 78, 88, 98.
- **Stratified random sampling** is also popular. This type is not concerned with equal probability of selection. Instead, the sociologist requires the sample to mirror the social characteristics of the population in terms of age, social class, gender and ethnicity. The sociologist therefore organises the potential research population into sampling frames that reflect these variables and applies systematic sampling to them. For example, a population of 500 might be divided into 250 men and 250 women and two samples of 25 may be randomly selected from each group.
- **Multi-stage sampling** involves selecting a sample from another sample, e.g. in opinion polls before an election, constituencies are chosen and individuals picked at random from these areas.
- **Cluster sampling** occurs when a sampling frame or list is not available. Some sociologists choose clusters of households by selecting areas or streets from a map at random.

Sampling does not always take a random form. Sometimes sampling frames do not exist for particular groups, especially those labelled deviant or unconventional. The need to get responses from particular types of people may override the scientific objectivity that underpins most random forms of sampling. The most common types of **non-random sampling** are as follows:

- **Quota sampling** is normally used when sociologists have a very clear idea of the sample they want and where to find it. For example, you may decide to investigate how students feel about your school or college by randomly selecting a particular dinnertime and handing out questionnaires to all those students who are in the canteen on that day. In other words, you know the canteen is going to contain a quota of people with the social characteristics you are interested in. There is always the danger with this type of sampling that you only include people who you know will give you the sorts of answers you are seeking, i.e. your friends or fellow sociologists. You need to avoid this temptation.
- Some sociologists use **purposive sampling**, i.e. they have a clear idea of particular untypical groups that they want to study because they want to test a specific hypothesis. For example, you may want to study boys' behaviour in bottom-stream mathematics groups. You will therefore target only this type of pupil, because they constitute an important part of your hypothesis.
- A popular sampling method used by sociologists who are researching deviant or criminal groups is **snowball** or **opportunity sampling**. Sampling frames of social groups such as drug-users are unlikely to exist, but access to a drug-user may lead to them introducing you to other drug-users willing to cooperate with your study. However, sociologists using this type of sampling technique can never be sure that their contacts are representative of the deviant or criminal population they are studying.

Key concepts

sampling frame; random sampling; non-random sampling; representativeness; generalisability

Operationalisation

This refers to the need for sociologists to transform a research question or hypothesis into something that can be measured through research. It means producing measurable and observable questions for a questionnaire and interview or categories for an observation or content analysis schedule. There are a number of considerations which influence this process. The **subject matter** of the research is going to influence the choice of research method. For example, can the subject matter be researched using methods that produce statistical data? Does the subject matter demand methods that explore the meaning behind human action and behaviour? Is the subject matter sensitive or embarrassing? The chosen **hypothesis** needs to be a clear statement, based on careful research and thinking, which makes a causal link between two variables. The hypothesis is either verified or refuted by the research findings.

The research population often needs to be operationalised in terms of social class, age, gender and ethnicity. It is important to be precise when identifying your population. For example, what do you mean by 'young people'? Do you mean children, teenagers or people in their twenties? Moreover, you will need to justify your choice in terms of your hypothesis.

Social class is often central to a research hypothesis and it is important to make clear how you are operationalising this concept. For many years, both the government and sociologists used job type as the basis for social class (see the Registrar General's categories of jobs and classes) but since 2000 social class has been operationalised by asking people questions relating to the nature of their employment (Are you an employer or employed? Are you full-time, part-time or temporary? Do you exercise authority over others? etc.) and their work situation (How much do you earn? etc.).

Ethnicity is a problematic concept and requires careful thought in regard to its operationalisation. For example, if you intend to study 'Asians', you will need to be precise in terms of country of origin, religion, etc. Terms like 'black' and 'white' will require some discussion to make your precise intentions clear.

The hypothesis itself will need to be broken down into its measurable components. If you have used any sociological terms such as 'cultural capital' or 'alienation', these will need to be clearly defined and questions constructed which measure aspects of them. For example, 'cultural capital' may require questions concerning the material supports that parents offer, e.g. books, computers, finance, own room, but also about cultural supports, e.g. encouragement to go on to university, parental tastes in music and literature. All the questions asked will need to be justified in terms of the context of cultural capital or whatever your central concepts are.

You will also need to think through how you might ask about sensitive topics like racism. Such topics might require the use of attitudinal scales such as 'On a scale of 1–5, 1 being "strongly agree" and 5 being "strongly disagree", consider the following list of statements', or it might simply be made up of a list of positive and negative statements which you ask respondents to tick. Whatever method is used, you need to state clearly what you are hoping to achieve by using these particular statements and how they relate to your hypothesis.

If you are using an observation schedule, it is important to justify the categories you are hoping to observe. For example, you may have a hypothesis that links male underachievement in schools to classroom behaviour. You will therefore need to operationalise male classroom behaviour by identifying categories of behaviour which are clearly different and problematic compared with conformist pupils. This may involve the construction of 'tally sheets' or diagrams of classroom organisation that allow you to map interaction between teachers and pupils (e.g. who asks questions, who gets told off most frequently) and between different pupils (e.g. who talks to whom, who misbehaves with whom).

If you are using a content analysis schedule or semiotic analysis, it is important that the categories or interpretations that you apply to media language/headlines or a particular media image operationalise your hypothesis accurately. For example, if you claim that the content of tabloid newspapers is sexist and patriarchal, it is essential that you identify those aspects of tabloid media content, e.g. language, headlines, photographs, features, advertisements, that you intend to investigate whilst stating how you expect that aspect to be sexist, e.g. language used may describe females in terms of their 'attractiveness' whilst males are described only in terms of their occupational status.

Ethical issues in research design

Whether you are studying Unit 2537 or Unit 2538, you need to be familiar with the ethics, i.e. moral issues associated with research. It is not just in the social sciences that ethical matters arise. In sociology, we encounter many situations that make us ask ourselves: 'What is the right course of action here?'

The **British Sociological Association** (BSA) suggests a number of ethical guidelines that should be adopted when doing sociological research:

- The well-being, rights and interests of the respondent must be protected.
- Informed consent should be sought.
- The research must be done on the basis of free participation and withdrawal.
- Confidentiality, privacy and anonymity should be guaranteed.
- Researchers need to consider the effects of the research on the respondents.
- Pseudonyms should be used.
- People who are ill, very young, very elderly or frail should be treated with special consideration.
- The BSA is particularly concerned about the use of ethnographic methods such as covert observation because such methods involve a degree of deception: the researcher hides his or her true identity and consequently people are misled and manipulated. The BSA is not keen on the use of this method and recommends that if it is used, the subjects of the research should be informed about the research when it has been concluded and their consent should be sought at that stage.

Other ethical considerations

- Research into crime and deviance can be ethically compromising because it may involve receiving information about criminal activities.
- Sometimes the research focus of the sociological study, e.g. rape or fear of crime, has the potential to cause anxiety, upset and grief and therefore needs to be sensitively thought through and handled, especially in terms of the design of the research device.
- Some sociologists believe that taking ethical risks is worthwhile because it may be the only valid way of gaining access to the data needed.

- For the student researcher at A2, such ethically compromising situations should not generally arise because the trust between you and your respondents should be paramount. You must remain accountable to them. (Remember too that if your respondents are young, the permission of their parents should be obtained before the research proceeds.)
- Student researchers need to give special thought to their own safety. You should never engage in research which puts you at risk in any way. No matter how appealing a 'risky' research strategy might be, you should always opt for a safer one. You will still generate valid sociological information.

Key concepts

operationalisation; hypothesis; ethics; social class; ethnicity

Data-collecting techniques

When sociologists talk about **primary methods**, they are referring to those which generate new data or knowledge, i.e. data that did not exist before the research was carried out. In contrast, **secondary methods/sources** provide evidence and information which have already been gathered by another researcher or organisation. Some studies use a combination of both types of data-gathering whilst others rely on either primary or secondary approaches.

Primary methods

Surveys

The social or sample survey is the most popular of all research methods. It normally involves the random selection of a representative large-scale sample (although surveys may be possible for small numbers too). This sample may be sent standardised questionnaires through the post and/or asked to take part in structured interviews in order to obtain large amounts of quantitative data (although sometimes qualitative data, especially relating to attitudes, can be collected in this way too). Surveys generally document opinions or attitudes, but some aim to identify correlations and make causal links. The survey is seen by scientific sociologists as having a number of strengths:

- If sampling is carried out without bias, i.e. randomly, and questionnaires are objectively designed, the social survey is thought to be the sociological equivalent of the laboratory method because all variables are controlled.
- It is thought to be a highly reliable method because it is easily repeated. Other sociologists can verify the data obtained by using the same standardised questionnaire and similar samples.

- It is seen to be objective because the sample population is randomly rather than deliberately selected, i.e. the sociologist's own preferences should not have polluted the sample.
- It generates lots of quantifiable data, i.e. statistics, in a relatively short period of time, relatively cheaply compared with other methods, especially if questionnaires are the primary research device.

Longitudinal surveys

This type of survey is sometimes called a 'panel study' or a 'cohort study' and goes on for a number of years. The key advantage of this approach is that it can reflect social change within the sample, whereas a traditional survey cannot. The researcher will return to the group at set intervals, and life-patterns can be analysed. A longitudinal survey provides an in-depth and therefore qualitative picture of a group or social trends. Regular contact over years can create trust and rapport between a group and the researchers and produce data which may be more valid than those generated by one-off questionnaires or interviews.

Survey questionnaires

A questionnaire is a set of questions, on paper (though internet or e-mail versions are increasingly common), which respondents are asked to complete. Data are gathered by means of fixed questions or items such as lists of statements with which people are asked to agree or disagree. Questionnaires are normally standardised, i.e. everyone who fills in the questionnaire is exposed to the same stimulus in the form of the same questions or statements. It is important that questionnaires begin with a brief introduction from the researcher, explaining the purpose of the survey, followed by a clear set of instructions about how the respondent should relate to the items. It is usually a good idea to guarantee confidentiality and anonymity to your respondents; this will greatly improve your chances of a high response rate. Bear in mind the following points about questionnaires and how they are designed:

- A questionnaire can be **direct**, i.e. it may be received directly from a researcher who waits for the respondent to fill it in or collects it later, or **indirect**, i.e. it may be sent through the post or via e-mail.
- Well-designed questionnaires often have a variety of items on them. For example, as well as open-ended items, fixed-response items and multiple-choice items (all of which will probably be in question form), they may also use ranking exercises which involve the scaling of responses such as 'strongly agree', 'disagree', etc. to a set of statements.
- Ranking scales are particularly useful when you are trying to find out about attitudes, opinions or views on controversial issues such as blood sports because they allow you to locate these on a spectrum or scale of viewpoints.
- It is worth remembering that you should always design items to do a particular job, and not be locked into using only open-ended or fixed-response items.
- Sequencing of items is also important in the design of questionnaires — it is usual

to start with a small number of fixed-response items designed to gather factual information, e.g. sex, age, ethnicity, followed by items that are slightly more open-ended, giving the respondent the chance to elaborate on how they feel, etc.
- The further the respondent gets into the research device, the more opportunity there should be to write about experiences, emotions and opinions.
- Be aware that too many items will put respondents off and could possibly lead to a low response rate.

Designing a questionnaire

There are certain types of question that should be avoided:
- **Ambiguous questions** — it is crucial that each question is open to one interpretation alone and that it has the same meaning for all people taking part in the survey.
- **Loaded questions** — emotional or sensitive questions which may provoke negative and invalid responses.
- **Leading questions** — be careful not to direct the respondent in a particular way.
- **Presuming questions** — you must not assume the respondent thinks or does something.
- **Double questions** — do not put together two separate questions which may require separate answers — make two clear questions.
- **Technical questions** — stick to ordinary language and don't assume the respondent understands technical jargon.
- **Vague questions** — avoid vague terms like 'generally', 'sometimes', 'seldom' — they mean different things to different people.

Key concepts

social survey; variables; standardisation; objectivity; quantifiability; longitudinal; panel study; cohort study; open and closed questions; response rate; leading and loaded questions

Evaluation

+ Surveys allow large amounts of data to be collected at a relatively low cost.
+ Questionnaire surveys can be done over a large geographical area and, if the sampling method adopted is efficient, they can be highly representative of the population, therefore giving a national or community picture.
+ Some sociologists regard large surveys as offering high levels of reliability because they are scientific in nature, exposing respondents to the same standardised stimulus.
+ The anonymity of respondents can be ensured, thus improving the response rate, especially when the study involves a sensitive topic, e.g. sexual attitudes or behaviour.
+ Once the questionnaire is distributed, the sociologist cannot influence the respondent.
+ If the items are pre-coded, the results are quite easy to analyse and tabulate and therefore have comparative value.
– Many questionnaire surveys, especially the postal variety, suffer from very low

response rates because there is no motivation for respondents to send them back.
- Sociologists often criticise this method because it does not allow the respondent to explain his or her experiences, motives, etc. to the researcher in any significant detail.
- Respondents might misunderstand items, no matter how carefully they have been designed, and this will lower the validity of the survey.
- With postal questionnaires, it is difficult to verify the identity of the person completing the form.
- The sample in a longitudinal survey may move away, die or refuse to take part the longer the study goes on. For example, many of the original sample involved in the television survey '7 Up' have now dropped out.

Studies which have used the survey method include *Poverty in the UK* (1979) by Peter Townsend, which did a great deal to convince people that poverty had not been abolished in the affluent 1960s as many believed. *A Nation of Home Owners* (1990) by Peter Saunders examined the growth of owner–occupancy in the UK and the implications for society, and *Social Class in Modern Britain* (1988) by Gordon Marshall et al. took a random sample of 1,315 adults in the UK and asked questions about social class, attitudes and behaviour.

Variations on the questionnaire

Self-report studies are questionnaires which are used by researchers in crime and deviance. They are 'questionnaires with a difference', in that they invite people to admit to crimes they have committed. It has been found that this type of device can permit respondents to disclose a range of offences that might not have been recorded by the police. Anonymity obviously has to be ensured, and validity is clearly an issue with this type of device and strategy (people might exaggerate or understate their offences), but they can give the sociologist a more complete picture of levels of law-breaking.

Victim studies are similar, in some ways, to self-report studies. They are questionnaires which give an insight into the rates, types and patterns of crimes of which people have been victims. Many crimes are not reported to the police by the victims, so this type of questionnaire can disclose information which would not appear in the official statistics. Obviously, the researcher has to ensure anonymity to respondents, as well as being sensitive to the ethical issues raised by asking people to recall unpleasant experiences.

Interviewing

A method which is clearly related to questionnaires, but is also very different in key respects, is interviewing. The relationship between researcher and respondent in interviews is face-to-face. In certain types of interview, the researcher 'probes' the attitudes and experiences of the respondent in a way which no other method will allow.

Structured or formal interviews involve the interviewer using an interview schedule on which fixed, pre-coded items are written. The items are standardised for all respondents and allow no freedom for the researcher to elaborate or make changes. The researcher records the answers given by the respondent. This could be done manually, or it could involve the use of a tape recorder (though some respondents are uncomfortable about their responses being recorded). If the latter approach is taken, it is necessary to transcribe the responses onto a recording sheet later. Sociologists often use both methods. This allows the researcher to ensure that he or she does not misinterpret or miss valuable information from the respondent. (If manual recording alone is used, this is a real possibility.)

Unstructured or informal interviews involve the interviewer using a series of items which mark out the main areas to explore in the interview. However, these items will usually be worded in a general way, i.e. as informal, open-ended questions. In addition to these questions researchers will use 'prompts' which aim to move the discussion into interesting areas arising from comments made by the respondent. The objective of such interviews is to allow the interviewee to respond freely and in depth; the sociologist's own priorities or interpretations should not be imposed on the interview process. Trust and rapport can be developed because the respondent can see that his or her input is valued and this may generate more qualitative and valid information about the respondent's interpretation of the world. Unstructured interviews also allow the researcher to probe for deeper meanings than in structured interviews. In many ways this style of interviewing is like a structured or guided conversation, in which the respondent can shape (to some degree) the direction the interview takes.

Semi-structured interviews tend to be made up of a combination of closed questions, usually gaining factual information about the respondent, and open questions, usually aimed at eliciting attitudinal information.

Evaluation

+ Interviews ensure a good response rate, provided rapport and trust is established between sociologist and respondent.
+ Personal and sensitive areas of experience can be researched, and detailed information can be gathered in semi-structured and unstructured interviews.
+ Deviant groups which are not open to study by other methods such as questionnaires may respond more positively to unstructured interviews because they have a chance to present their own viewpoint.
+ High levels of validity are obtained from unstructured interview data because sociologists are gathering first-hand accounts and interpretations.
+ The researcher can explain/elaborate on areas for discussion in semi-structured and unstructured interviews if the respondent seeks clarification.
– Interviews can be time-consuming, especially if semi-structured or unstructured.
– Interviewing can be expensive, especially in a large-scale survey, because interviewers need to be recruited, trained and paid.
– Research using interviews generally involves small samples (because of the expense and the time-consuming nature of this method), so generalisations to wider populations may not be possible because of the unrepresentative nature of interview samples.

- Inaccurate and incomplete recording of respondent comments can mean unreliable research and invalid findings.

Focus-group interviews have recently become popular with sociologists. These are a type of group interview made up of between four and ten people led by a 'facilitator' or leader who guides the topic being discussed with questions worked out beforehand. Focus-group members are encouraged to talk to and respond to each other rather than to the facilitator, thus allowing people to explore their attitudes and experiences in their own words. Such groups also include an 'observer' who notes the organisation of the room and the dynamics of the interaction.

Evaluation

+ If facilitators are skilled at group management, trust and rapport should be achieved in a secure and comfortable environment which produces valid data.
+ Focus groups not only measure the extent of an opinion, but can also investigate the reasons why it was formed.
+ Focus groups result in qualitative data expressed in the words of the participants.
- Focus groups are not generally representative of particular social groups.
- Focus groups may not be representative of the general population because strong personalities may dominate and silence dissent.

Interview bias or effect

All types of interview suffer from bias or effect, which can affect the validity of data. If you are using interviews in coursework or considering this method as part of your response to an examination context, it is important that you consider the following characteristics of interview bias or effect in some detail:

- When sociologists conduct interviews, and also when they process their data, they need to be sensitive to the fact that they might be acting in a **selective** way without realising it. Decisions regarding which comments from your respondent you consider most significant, and which statements/quotes you decide not to include in your final report, may reflect subjective bias on your part rather than objective selection. Sociologists are only human!
- A power imbalance is automatically built into a social situation where one person interviews another, which may undermine the validity of research findings. For example, some people may find interviews threatening because they are not sure about the motives of the interviewer. Others may associate interviewers with officialdom, authority and possible punishment and consequently might not cooperate fully. They may withhold certain crucial information about their behaviour and attitudes.
- The interviewer's social identity and status may affect the interview process. Ethnicity, age, sex and even social class (demonstrated by accent or dress) may play a part in how well (or badly) the interview goes. For example, teenagers may interpret adult interviewers asking about aspects of illegal delinquent behaviour as threatening and consequently fail to cooperate fully in terms of the quality and validity of information offered.

- Even those who do not feel threatened by the research will search for clues from the interviewer and the questions about how they ought to be behaving. These 'demand characteristics' may mean that respondents adjust their behaviour in order to influence the way in which the interviewer sees them.
- The 'social desirability' effect is one effect of demand characteristics. It involves the over-reporting of 'desirable' things such as giving to charity and the under-reporting of 'undesirable' things such as racist behaviour.
- Another problem with interviews arises from human nature. Many people engage in yea-saying — tending to agree rather than disagree, to be satisfied rather than dissatisfied, etc.
- When interviews, of whatever type, are carried out the researcher needs to pay careful attention and be sensitive to non-verbal communication cues such as body language which reveal the reaction of the respondent to the issues being discussed. The body language of the interviewer may also reveal a particular viewpoint on an issue and affect the quality and validity of the response of the interviewee. Researchers should attempt to strike a neutral position on the topics being discussed.
- The location of the interview needs to be one in which all your respondents feel comfortable and should not be too formal in its organisation.
- The pace and timing of questioning needs to be sensitive to the interviewee; otherwise he or she may become alienated and non-communicative.
- Guaranteeing anonymity and confidentiality may help minimise interview bias.

Key concepts

structured interviews; unstructured interviews; interviewer bias or effect; validity; focus groups; subjectivity; bias; social identity; social desirability effect; yea-saying; demand characteristics

Studies which have used this method include *Homeworking Women* (Phizacklea and Wolkowicz, 1995) which examined aspects of daily home-based work for women from various ethnicities in different types of job. The *Living with Heroin* study (Parker et al. 1988) used interviews to find out why young people in the Wirrall used heroin.

Pilot studies

Most of the problems with questionnaires and interviews can be minimised by carrying out a pilot study. This small-scale prototype of the main study can act as a 'dress rehearsal' and provide guidance on the following areas:

- whether your sampling frame is suitable
- the potential non-response from your target audience
- the clarity of your questionnaire or interview schedule
- whether your questions should be open or closed, e.g. in order to collect all possible answers for a closed question in the main survey, you could have it open in the pilot
- the effectiveness of the interviewers

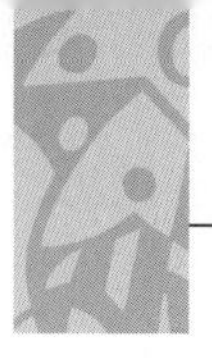

Observation

With this method the researcher 'stands outside' the group or social situation being studied and works 'at a distance'. The aim of such sociologists is to get inside the head of those being studied and to see the world through their eyes. This is *verstehen*, i.e. the researcher intends to empathise with those being studied, to understand their motives, their attitudes and the social meanings or interpretations they attach to everyday life. For example, a sociologist might be interested in how people behave in everyday contexts such as bus queues. You might find it odd that a bus queue should be considered worthy of sociological attention, but in all social situations there are rules and expectations. Body language, issues of 'territory' and personal space, and matters relating to eye contact — all these are in operation as people wait for the Number 33! There is, in other words, a 'structure of expected interaction'. A sociologist attempting to analyse and understand this would certainly select observation as his or her main method. A notebook, tally-chart or observation grid would be employed to record behaviour and the researcher would obviously need to avoid detection. A subtle style of recording is vital, so as not to influence the group's behaviour. The following general points about observation methods can be made:

- This method allows the researcher *some* access to the world of the group being studied and is therefore what sociologists call an **ethnographic** approach.
- The researcher usually carries out a pilot observation to identify the 'fields' or categories of observation, i.e. what specific aspects of the situation are most worthy of study.
- The pilot observation will help determine how much factual detail to record about the members of the group being observed (e.g. age, sex) and what names or numbers to give to them so that their behaviour can be recorded effectively.
- Once the research has been carried out, the sociologist's urgent task is to analyse the recorded details whilst images and memories are still fresh in the mind.

The **sociogram** is a method sometimes used in the study of children, particularly in an observational educational setting. It involves the researcher drawing diagrams which represent, for example, patterns of friendship and interaction within a classroom, e.g. who sits where, and with whom. Different sub-groups can then be observed and their educational progress perhaps correlated with their friendship patterns.

Evaluation

+ This method is regarded as producing valid data because the researcher is detached from 'the action' and is therefore unlikely to distort the group's behaviour.
+ Observation operates in the natural environment of those being studied. In this sense, it is less artificial than questionnaires or interviews.
+ People may not be aware that they are behaving in certain ways. Questionnaires and interviews can only uncover conscious behaviour, while observation may reveal people acting in ways that they would deny if asked directly.
+ The researcher is unlikely to lose objectivity because of the detached nature of this method.

- Observation is time-consuming — research of this nature often takes months, even years.
- The selectivity of the researcher can present problems. A vast amount of behaviour is observed and the sociologist has to make decisions about which behaviour does or does not support the research hypothesis, opening the way for accusations of bias.
- However well access to the group has been managed, the presence of a researcher may disrupt the natural behaviour of the group and create artificial reactions.
- Some aspects of group behaviour may be difficult to interpret or understand, especially if the sociologist is not involved in the group and has no access to the perspective of its members.
- The sociologist's interpretation of the data may be compromised by the fact that he or she likes the group and therefore is unable to judge their actions objectively.

Key concepts

ethnography; participant observation; covert observation; *verstehen*

Studies which have used this method include *The Rules of Disorder* (Marsh, 1982) observing the behaviour of groups of soccer fans on the terraces and *The Making of Men* (Mac An Ghaill, 1994) concerning schooling and masculinities.

Participant observation

The second form of observation is one in which the sociologist actually joins the social group being studied, i.e. participant observation. Many sociologists claim that this particular method has a high level of validity because the sociologist experiences first-hand the worldview of those he or she is studying.

Participant observation is usually the only way of obtaining detailed information about groups which traditionally 'shut out' or exclude social researchers, e.g. deviant groups whose members follow a lifestyle and subscribe to a value-system which is very different from and possibly opposed to mainstream values.

There are two broad types of participant observation:

- **Overt participant observation** is when the sociologist spends extended periods of time living with a group but has made it clear to its members that she or he is not a 'standard' group-member, and does not want to adopt the style of the group or its values, but is simply a person doing some research. (It is not usually necessary or advisable to label oneself 'a sociologist', which can be daunting.) This type of participant observation permits questions to be asked about the way the group does things whenever new situations arise. The researcher has 'owned up' to the fact that she or he is an outsider, so questions are not out of place. Equally, the researcher is at liberty to record openly things she or he considers of sociological significance, and the group members will not see this as odd. This type of participant observation has one major drawback: the presence of a researcher within the group may distort or inhibit the group's behaviour.

- **Covert participant observation** involves living with a group, but this time the sociologist 'goes undercover' and hides the fact that she or he is doing research. This has the advantage of allowing the sociologist to study the group when its members are behaving naturally and therefore increases the validity of data collected. However, the researcher has a great deal of learning to do in order to fit into the group. The body language, style of dress, slang or language, customs and rituals of the group will have to be learned. Many sociologists gain access to groups through an intermediary — somebody who can vouch for them. Once access has been gained the researcher faces the challenge of recording events effectively without raising suspicions.

Reflexivity

This concept, which is particularly associated with the ethnographic approach, refers to the process by which sociologists periodically review the degree of detachment or objectivity they have achieved in a research project, their rapport with the respondents and the way they process data, etc. in order to ensure methodological integrity.

Evaluation

+ Participant observation, whether overt or covert, allows access to 'exclusive' data and natural behaviour in contrast with other methods such as questionnaires or interviews which produce more artificial behaviour.
+ Participant observation data, especially when gathered by covert observation, result in high levels of validity because people are behaving naturally rather than reacting to being watched — this latter type of behaviour is known as the Hawthorne effect after a famous observation conducted in the 1930s at the Hawthorne plant of the General Electric Company in which it was realised that workers were working harder because they were being observed.
+ Participant observation often gives rise to new ideas for study as a direct result of researchers being involved with groups, i.e. they see things which they might not have asked about if they had been using questionnaires or interviews.
+ Because the research is ongoing, it gives a picture of the group as dynamic (changing) rather than static, which adds a special quality and validity to the information gathered.
– Participant observation can be extremely time-consuming and expensive — some studies have lasted for 5 years.
– There can be ethical problems because there is a risk of the researcher being drawn into illegal behaviour when studying criminal groups — the question arises whether the researcher should 'break cover' and refuse to participate or stay covert and hope the behaviour does not get too deviant.
– Researchers conducting observations can be exposed to danger.
– Another ethical problem is that 'informed consent' is not obtained from those being observed, and many argue that this makes the sociologist guilty of deceiving and misleading respondents, and betraying their trust.
– There is also the danger that researchers can become too involved in the life of

the group. Some sociologists have been known to 'go native' and lose their sense of objectivity and detachment, therefore potentially lowering the validity of any data gathered.

- Some sociologists argue that the reliability of observation is low because it is not based on a standardised scientific approach — it is dependent upon the strength of the unique personal relationships that the researcher establishes with those being observed, which cannot be replicated by other sociologists.
- Participant observation studies tend to focus on small, exotic or deviant groups which may not be representative of society, so generalisability from any results may be low (although observation studies are often presented as case studies which do not aim to generalise).
- Final conclusions are always based on the subjective and selective interpretations of a single researcher who chooses what to include in the published findings.

Studies which have used this method in its overt form include *The Girls in the Gang* (Campbell, 1984), a study of female delinquency, and *Doing the Business* (Hobbs, 1995), which was an ethnographic study of petty criminals and the police. Studies which have used this method in its covert form include *Tearoom Trade* (Humphries, 1970), a study of homosexual activity, and *Inside the British Police* (Holdaway, 1984), a study of police practices and attitudes by a serving police officer doing a sociology degree.

Key concepts

ethnography; participant observation; covert observation; sociogram; reflexivity; objectivity; Hawthorne effect; going native

Experiments

It is not just the natural sciences that use experiments; the social sciences have their own variations on 'experimental method'. Experiments in sociology are carried out in naturally occurring settings and are referred to as **social** or **field experiments**. By manipulating one particular variable or potential influence in a familiar social context the sociologist can test out the reactions of respondents (who, of course, are not aware that a social experiment is taking place), e.g. Garfinkel asked students to act as formal lodgers in their own homes to gauge the effect of a change in children's behaviour on parents. This type of sociological research is clearly related to the interpretive approach, and examines the way people behave in everyday, small social groups.

Evaluation

+ Social experiments allow the sociologist to 'unravel' the (often hidden) processes and rules of everyday social life.
+ Experiments enable the researcher to get very close to people's interpretations of everyday experiences.
- Most experiments do not involve the informed consent of those being experimented upon and some concern has been expressed about ethical issues such as deception and manipulation of respondents.

- This method can be risky for the researcher if respondents react badly when they discover that they have been involved in an experiment.
- There may be a 'Hawthorne effect', i.e. people's behaviour may be the result of the experiment or the presence of the researchers rather than the product of the variables under investigation.

Studies which have used this method include *Pygmalion in the Classroom* (Rosenthal and Jacobson, 1968), a study of how teacher labels affect pupil performance. Another experiment was *On Being Sane in Insane Places* (Rosenhahn, 1973) in which students were asked to present themselves at a mental hospital and fake the symptoms of mental illnesses in order to be admitted and test out the labelling processes operating in such institutions.

Log books/time-budget diaries

This method involves the respondents themselves recording their activities and interactions over a set period of time using grids in time-budget diaries or log books. Note the following key points:

- This method is particularly useful in the area of the domestic division of labour — husband and wife log books may be a more valid way of generating data about who does what in the household than questionnaire surveys.
- The sociologist needs to decide just how much of the respondent's daily experiences can reasonably be entered into the log book. There is a risk of the respondent becoming irritated if she or he is asked to do so much recording that the task becomes tedious.
- It is also important to give respondents a trial period with the log book so that they become used to the layout of the grids and the idea of recording significant events regularly.
- The sociologist always needs to give a lot of thought to the way in which central issues in the research are operationalised, or 'built into' the research device. Will the device deliver the desired type of data?

Key concepts

social experiments; field experiments; variables; time-budgeting

Evaluation

+ Diaries may generate genuine and therefore valid insight into an individual's daily life.
+ This method is very cheap.
+ The individual records what the respondent sees as significant, and for interpretivists this gives a particular value to the data gathered because the sociologist's interpretation is not imposed on the reality being researched.
+ The method generates data which are more than just a 'snapshot' — they give a continuous and evolving picture of social events.
- This is a highly subjective method — the respondent alone selects what is to be recorded and has to be trusted to tell the truth.
- Respondents often lose interest in the recording process and the reliability of the data can decline as time goes on, undermining the validity of the final product.

Part-primary/part-secondary methods

Content analysis

This method is seen by some as a secondary method, but in reality it involves working with secondary data but generating new knowledge. For this reason it can also be seen as a primary method.

It involves the analysis of patterns or 'messages' in the mass media and can generate both quantitative and qualitative data. The sociologist can work with any form of media product, e.g. newspapers, television programmes or magazines, and also with other cultural products such as novels. The aim of the research, in general, is to identify how particular social groups or social situations are portrayed in the product being analysed. There are a number of key elements you should note:

- The quantitative form of this method involves a 'tallying' or counting approach and uses a grid that records the patterns and frequency of certain images. For example, the sociologist studying images of masculinity and femininity in the workplace as depicted in Australian soap operas on television will systematically record frequencies of images, representations, categories, etc.
- The qualitative form of this method known as **semiology** or **textual analysis** involves analysing language, images, narrative, etc. for ideological content, i.e. asking whether the product reflects a dominant political or cultural position. Semiologists argue that these ideological messages might be about femininity, national pride or race, but whatever they deal with, they are subconsciously absorbed by society in everyday 'reading' of images and words.
- The validity of content analysis is increased by a trialling phase in which all potential categories or fields of observation are identified in order to refine the research device.
- The final research device must have a design or shape which structures the observation, but which also allows some flexibility in case the researcher finds unexpected patterns and events.
- The sociologist needs to select the sample carefully. Just as a researcher using questionnaires needs to decide who is going to be in the sample population, so in content analysis the selection of, say, magazines or television programmes needs to be justified. For example, a researcher looking at television advertising needs to think very carefully about which channels are to be sampled, at what time of day, etc.
- If you intend to use this method, you need to be realistic. For example, if you have decided to research how tabloid newspapers deal with controversial issues such as euthanasia, compared with broadsheet newspapers, you need to be certain that there is enough coverage of that particular topic in the newspapers at the time when you are due to do your research.

Key concepts

content analysis; semiology; textual analysis; ideological content

Evaluation

+ Content analysis is cheap.
+ If a longitudinal comparative version is used, it allows the sociologist to compare depictions and representations over a period of time.
- This is a very time-consuming method.
- It can often be highly subjective, e.g. semiotics largely depends upon the interpretation of the researcher. Different researchers may interpret the same images, etc. in different ways.
- Sociologists who have used this method have been accused of taking an image or set of words out of context and misinterpreting the meaning.
- Using this method often means assuming that these media images, representations, etc. have an effect upon their audience. However, there is no proof of this.

Studies which have used this method include *Bad News* (1976) by the Glasgow Media Group which suggested that industrial disputes and business matters are reported in a biased way, and *Forever Feminine* (Ferguson, 1983) which detailed various images of femininity in magazines.

Case studies

When a sociologist uses the case study approach it is usually in order to study in depth a particular organisation, a small group of respondents or community sharing similar experiences, or an individual, e.g. a delinquent.

With an organisational case study, the sociologist might study a factory or a school with the aim of getting inside the 'life' of the institution in question using a multiple-methods approach called **methodological pluralism**. For example, for a case study of a factory, the sociologist might interview the shop-floor workers in order to find out about their levels of loyalty to the company. She or he might also use participant observation to look at and record incidents of conflict and dispute between workers and management, as well as issuing a questionnaire to a sample of employees at all levels of the factory in order to establish what levels of job satisfaction people had in different types of work. Once all of these data were analysed and interpreted, the sociologist would have a comprehensive insight into the social life of the organisation.

The other type of case study involves in-depth analysis of the experiences and views of a small sample of individuals with similar experiences. For example, the sociologist might study a small group of individuals who had all been victims of violent crime in order to find out how respondents had altered their lifestyles as a result of their experiences. In order to carry out this research, the method of semi-structured interviews could be used. In addition, the case-study approach usually necessitates repeated interviews, over a period of time, which gives more depth and also the possibility of recording changes that occur in the respondent's life, attitudes, etc. In some circumstances, the sociologist would try to gain access to any personal documents, e.g. letters and diaries, that might give insight into the life experiences or life history of the respondents, or might ask people to keep diaries recording their fears about crime.

Evaluation

+ Case studies often result in a high degree of insight into people's experiences.
+ They are relatively cheap to carry out.
+ They offer respondents the chance to give an insight into their emotions as well as their experiences.
+ The case study stresses the viewpoints and interpretations of those being studied and therefore scores highly in terms of validity.
– The organisation or group being studied may not be typical or representative of society as a whole, so generalisation from findings may not be possible (although sociologists conducting case studies often argue that their aims are quite different from those involved in a social survey).
– The reliability of data is sometimes questionable, especially when respondents are asked to remember past events.

Secondary methods and sources

Sociologists also use secondary data, i.e. information gathered by other sociologists or organisations. This pre-existing data can take a number of forms, most obviously **related studies**, i.e. books and articles that have something in common with the topic being studied. Over and above these sources, the sociologist will also make use of a range of evidence.

Official statistics

These are figures collected by government or state agencies. They are an example of quantitative data and are gathered through surveys by both national and local government agencies. They offer the sociologist a rich data bank to tap into and cover a range of aspects of the way we live as a society. The Office for National Statistics (ONS) is the agency in charge of official statistics in England and Wales.

Generally speaking, we can divide official figures into two categories: registration data and survey data.

Registration data

- This involves the recording (as a continuous process) of sociologically important events such as births, deaths, marriages and divorces. As a society, we have a highly developed system of registering, documenting and quantifying key social events. For example, the Department for Education and Skills (DfES) records truancy rates in schools in England and Wales.

Survey data

- This type of official statistic is gathered by specific social surveys which happen at particular times. These are often huge surveys of representative samples.

- The best example is the decennial census. Every ten years millions of questionnaires are filled in and valuable data gathered about life in Britain. The last census was in 2001 and it cost £254 million.
- On a more frequent basis, the *General Household Survey* and the *New Earnings Survey* provide annual information. Much of the data gathered by such surveys can be found in *Social Trends*.
- The *British Crime Survey* gathers information about how much crime has been reported by victims and is often used to cross-check the accuracy of the *official criminal statistics* which are made up of crimes reported to the police, crimes detected and convictions in the courts.

Key concepts

case study; methodological pluralism; official statistics; registration data; survey data; the census

Evaluation

+ Official statistics are extremely easy to access. See, for example, the government publication *Social Trends* or the website **www.statistics.gov.uk**
+ Official statistics are up to date.
+ They are often gathered by surveys which involve huge, carefully constructed representative samples and therefore can be generalised for similar populations.
+ Positivists see official statistics as 'hard' reliable facts because they have been collected in a standardised, systematic and scientific fashion. For example, registration data on birth, marriage, divorce and death are regarded as both highly reliable and valid because they are the outcome of long-standing and systematic procedures.
+ Trends can be identified by comparing official statistics from regularly conducted surveys, e.g. the census.
– Many official statistics do not 'speak for themselves' — they raise serious questions about reliability and validity.
– Official statistics may only give us a partial picture of a sociological problem. For example, the official crime statistics do not include unreported and undetected crimes.
– Official statistics may tell us more about the people involved in their collection than the social trend they claim to describe. For example, crime statistics may tell us more about police and judicial practices than about criminality, while suicide statistics may tell us more about social attitudes towards suicide and the practices of coroners than the motives of suicide victims.
– Statistics are one-dimensional in their validity, i.e. they tell us very little about the human stories or interpretations that underpin them. For example, divorce statistics express very little about the social experience of divorce.
– Official statistics are open to political abuse — they can be manipulated or 'massaged' by governments for political advantage. For example, the validity of unemployment and NHS waiting-list statistics may be undermined by frequent re-definitions by government or selective practices.

– Official statistics may be based on operational definitions that sociologists would not agree with. For example, the government may use absolute ways of defining poverty based on income levels whereas sociologists may prefer relative approaches to measuring poverty.

Studies which have used this source include *Suicide* (Durkheim, 1897), a classic study which used a comparative approach to identify different types of suicide and the variables that pre-disposed social groups to this act. *A Nation of Home Owners* (Saunders, 1990) used statistics to examine the growth of owner-occupancy in the UK and the implications for society.

Personal/expressive documents

Sociologists often try to gain access to the personal or expressive documents which record people's social experiences, e.g. letters and personal diaries (not to be confused with time-budget diaries). Bear in mind the following points about this type of data:

- Such 'life documents' offer the researcher a potentially rich source of qualitative data and an insight into the life history of an individual or group.
- In particular, these types of data can reveal the emotions, reflections and motivations of the research subjects, i.e. they are likely to be high in validity.
- Diaries and letters can give significant insight as people go through challenging social experiences such as bereavement, or social mobility into a new social stratum.
- They are favoured by the interpretive branch of sociology. Some feminist writers also consider them to be valuable.
- The sociologist should always obtain consent from the person who wrote the letters or diary (unless the person is deceased).

Key concepts

life documents; expressive documents; consent

Evaluation

+ Personal documents give rich, detailed and valid insight into challenging social experiences and emotions.
+ They often give insight over a long period of time, so social change can be examined.
+ They are often the only insight sociologists have into the past.
– The validity of data offered by such sources may be undermined by doubts about the documents' authenticity.
– There is selectivity in what the writer includes in such documents. Writers of diaries or letters are unlikely to include information that may prejudice the reader against them.
– Analysing such documents introduces a further degree of subjectivity. There is always the danger that the sociologist will interpret what a writer is saying in a different way to that which the writer intended.
– Such documents are not produced with sociological research in mind, so they may offer only a partial insight into the lifestyle in question.

- The experiences described are unlikely to be typical or representative because there is a tendency for only certain types of people, e.g. literary, political people in the public eye, to keep letters or write diaries about their experiences.

Studies which have used this approach include *The Polish Peasant in Europe and America* (Thomas and Znaniecki, 1919), a classic study of migration to the United States, and *The Company She Keeps* (Hey, 1997), a study of girls' friendships through their diaries and notes to each other. Students might also wish to refer to *Documents of Life* (Plummer, 1983).

Contemporary documents

Media products, such as newspapers, magazines, advertisements, radio, music products, posters, films, novels, internet and computer products, tell us something about the particular society in which we live. Sociologists often use media extracts or items to reflect the values, priorities or concerns in society at any one point in time. Equally, quality investigative journalism can generate reliable evidence which may complement the research of the sociologist.

Evaluation

+ Media products are interesting and useful to the sociologist if treated with caution.
+ They are cheap and readily available.
- A great deal of journalism is politically biased. Newspapers, in particular, openly support particular political parties and ideals and may lack objectivity.
- Media products can be unreliable because they may reflect the personal and political prejudices of media personnel such as journalists, editors and owners.
- The content of these products is not constructed or designed with sociological research in mind and may therefore lack sociological precision in terms of definition/operationalisation and measurement.

Historical documents

Historical records such as parish records, the census (which began in 1851) and government white papers on particular social problems give useful insights into the past.

Evaluation

+ Historical documents allow comparisons over time in order to identify trends.
+ They can help show the effectiveness (or otherwise) of social policy measures, e.g. the National Health system.
- Doubts about the authenticity of historical documents can undermine their validity.
- Historical statistics may not be comparable with modern ones because means of measurement may be more accurate in the modern age. For example, church attendance figures today are more precise than they were 100 years ago.

Studies which have used this method include *Hooligan* (Pearson, 1983), which demonstrates that the fear of social disorder from 'hooligans' has been with us for much longer than we often realise, and *The World We Have Lost* (Laslett, 1965), which examines how much family structures have changed over the centuries.

Pressure-group/think-tank data

Data gathered by organisations and groups which take a particular position on specific social issues are often controversial and provocative. However, they can be useful for the sociologist, provided that there is an awareness of the potential problems involved. There are many pressure groups, and also a number of think-tanks producing policy papers on social issues and problems such as juvenile crime and prisons. They often have a political standpoint and are linked to one of the major political parties. For example, the Institute for Economic Affairs (IEA) is generally seen as having a conservative political outlook.

Evaluation

+ Pressure groups/think-tanks often collect a wealth of information on social problems not immediately accessible to sociologists, e.g. on the effectiveness of prisons.
+ Such information is made available to sociologists at little cost.
– Pressure-group and think-tank data may be tainted with bias arising from political affiliation and vested interests. Although data are usually collected in a reliable way, the validity of the conclusions reached by such research may be questionable.

Triangulation

Triangulation can be defined as the use of more than one method of research in order to assess the validity of research methods and especially the data produced. This usually involves the use of a method which generates quantitative data — this may be primary data from a survey or secondary data from official sources. More often than not, this is combined with a more interactive method such as unstructured interviews or observation which generates qualitative data. A number of advantages in using this approach can be seen:

- It can be used to check the accuracy of the data gathered by each method. Often the emphasis on reliability in devices such as standardisation in questionnaires or structured interviews can reduce the validity of research data because people find such methods artificial or impersonal and tend not to be wholly honest or open. The use of a second, more qualitative device, e.g. unstructured interviews with a sub-sample, can serve to cross-check the validity of people's responses to a more quantitative method. Do they really act in the way they say they do? Qualitative data in the form of conversational analysis can sometimes be transformed into quantitative closed questions and fixed-choice responses which can be applied to much larger samples.
- Qualitative research can produce hypotheses which can be checked and researched using quantitative methods.
- The two approaches can give a more complete picture of the group being studied, i.e. they can be studied from a number of different angles.
- Qualitative research can focus on the 'why' and 'how' of the patterns and trends uncovered by statistics. For example, research on divorce can uncover both statistical trends and people's actual feelings about the experience of divorce.

- Eileen Barker's *The Making of a Moonie* (1984) (a study of a religious sect) is a good example of triangulation in practice.

Methodological pluralism refers to the employment of more than one research method, normally in a two-stage study in which both methods are given equal status rather than one being used to facilitate the other or one method being subordinated to the other. The emphasis is on building up a fuller and more comprehensive picture of social life by generating different types of data which shed light on different parts of the research problem. This differs from the classic form of triangulation which aims primarily to use one method in order to cross-check data from another.

Janet Finch and Jennifer Mason's *Negotiating Family Responsibilities* (1993) (which examined how family members supported each other) is a good example of methodological pluralism in practice.

Evaluation

+ Triangulation and methodological pluralism are useful because the advantages of one method may help compensate for and overcome (at least partially) the limitations of another.
+ For the professional researcher, there are few areas of social life where one research method alone is sufficient to gain a meaningful insight into people's lives.
– These approaches are expensive.
– They produce vast amounts of data which can be difficult to analyse.
– The nature of the topic to be investigated dictates which method(s) are employed and rules out others.

Questions & Answers

This section of the guide looks at the way you need to approach the **Applied Sociological Research Skills (2537)** exam by examining the style and content of the answers you should try to produce. Two questions in the style of the OCR unit test are provided, followed by grade-C and grade-A responses. Note that the grade-A answers are not 'perfect' answers. There are other ways of gaining a grade A, perhaps by using an alternative approach or different content. You might even come to different conclusions to the ones presented. However, the grade-A responses demonstrate some important strengths. First, they answer the question set. Next, they deliver the appropriate examinable skills. They use valid concepts, studies and writers. They also select, apply, analyse and interpret data effectively, and are structured logically. Finally, they demonstrate a clear ability to evaluate the material used. The grade-C responses may do some but not all of these things or they may deliver most of the skills but not very effectively. Students who achieve a grade C are on the right track, but they under-perform in some respects.

A third question is provided which is not accompanied by a student answer. It is followed by a plan of action, and you should use this to write your own response. It is recommended that you spend some time revising the topic before tackling this question. You should answer it under timed conditions with no notes.

Examiner's comments

The sample responses are accompanied by examiner's comments. These are preceded by the icon *e* and indicate where credit is due. For the grade-A answers, the examiner points out what it is that enables the candidates to score so highly. Particular attention is given to the use of the examinable skills mentioned above. For the grade-C answers, the examiner points out areas for improvement, specific problems and common errors. You might consider rewriting these answers in a way which would gain higher marks.

Question 1

Item A

Ghazala Bhatti's study, *Asian Children at Home and at School* (1999), is an ethnographic study of the home and the school experiences of a group of Asian children who attended 'Cherrydale School', a mixed comprehensive in 'Cherrytown' in the south of England. Detailed interviews with children, their parents and teachers were carried out individually and in groups, over a period of 2 years. These were supplemented by closed questionnaires and participant observation inside and outside the classroom. This methodological pluralism has a number of strengths. Qualitative methods like unstructured interviews and observation produce data based primarily on the first-hand experience of those being studied. In other words, the subjects' interpretation of reality is given priority and this can help limit the potential bias that might result if the researcher's own preconceived notions, stereotypes or prejudices were allowed to come into play. Moreover, the range of different groups being studied allowed Bhatti to study the same sociological problems from different angles or perspectives. She was also able to see the differences between people's stated intentions in interviews and questionnaires and their actual actions. Moreover, if a questionnaire is followed by observation and further analysis, the researcher can challenge the assumptions behind the questions he or she has asked in the first place, and even learn something about the limitations of the method.

Bhatti makes some interesting observations on being an Asian woman researcher. She noted that 'the research was affected by my age, sex and ethnic origin and my status as a researcher and the languages I could or could not speak. Often my status varied in relation to the person with whom I was interacting. Asian parents knew me as someone younger than them who had daily access to their children and their children's school. They realised that I was bilingual, and that I could be trusted with some confidential family matters. The teachers' responses to me varied and were somewhat contradictory. My status as a researcher who was never formally introduced to the school by the headteacher considerably diminished any potential threat I may have posed; at the same time my sex and ethnicity, that of a Pakistani woman, was a source of open curiosity and suspicion in some cases. Some teachers were very conscious of the close relationships I had with children, especially when I talked in Urdu and Punjabi with disruptive children. I sometimes took both my young children, neither of whom were of school age, with me on home visits to the Asian parents. Most of the parents accepted my wife/mother persona as a homely, non-threatening image. I was certainly not seen as a distant, middle-class, Asian, professional woman. Yet, I was of the same kin, did not live next door to the parents, did not regularly socialise with their friends and was not likely to spread gossip against them. This made me trustworthy.'

Adapted from G. Bhatti, *Asian Children at Home and at School* (Routledge, 1999).

(a) Using only Item A, identify *two* reasons why some sociologists prefer to use methodological pluralism. (6 marks)

(b) Identify and explain *two* problems in conducting longitudinal research over a period of years. (8 marks)

(c) Summarise, in your own words, what Item A tells us about how the social characteristics of a researcher may affect the validity of research findings. (10 marks)

Item B

The Commission for Racial Equality requires quantitative data about the reasons why African-Caribbean and Asian parents are sometimes reluctant to become involved in school activities such as parents' evenings, open days and parent–teacher association meetings. You have been asked, as a sociological researcher, to design a proposal which will target a representative sample of African-Caribbean and Asian parents in London, Birmingham, Bradford and Leeds.

(d) Outline and explain the research process you would adopt in collecting quantitative data on why parents in African-Caribbean and Asian communities may not participate in school activities. (14 marks)

(e) Assess the potential weaknesses of the research proposal, explaining briefly how you would intend to overcome them. (22 marks)

■ ■ ■

Answer to question 1: grade-C candidate

(a) A problem with some sociological research is that when researchers are examining their results, they might read too much into particular data and misinterpret them. Qualitative data from unstructured interviews allow researchers to make sure they are interpreting what they see correctly.

Secondly, she got a good range of viewpoints, i.e. teachers, children and parents, on the points she was interested in.

e The candidate distinguishes between two reasons why some sociologists use methodological pluralism. The first reason is explained fully with a clear illustration relating to unstructured interviews backing up observation data. The second reason is fairly clear but would benefit from an example illustrating the sociological point. The candidate would score 5 out of a possible 6 marks.

(b) First, longitudinal research over a period of years is going to be very expensive because the salaries of interviewers will have to be paid for a long time.

Second, there is always the danger that the sample will become fragmented as the years go by. In other words, the respondents might die or lose interest in the project. This happened in the '7-Up' television series which has followed a group of children from the age of 7 until the age of 42.

e Although two problems are identified, the first is not very strong sociologically because a researcher conducting longitudinal research will normally only do so if sufficient funding has been secured. The second problem is a sociological one but the candidate needs to discuss briefly the implications of the sample 'fragmenting' in order to make clear how it will affect the research. For example, the candidate might link it to non-response, representativeness or reliability. This answer would score 5 out of a possible 8 marks.

(c) Bhatti argues that the validity of her research findings was heavily influenced by her social characteristics in terms of her age, sex, ethnic origin, the languages she could speak and being a sociological researcher.

Asian parents seemed to like Bhatti because she was both an Asian and a mother. She found that if she took her young children along to interviews, people would find her 'non-threatening' and consequently they were willing to trust her and open up to her. This meant that her interview data were more valid because people were more willing to confide in someone who was very similar to them. Bhatti points out that if she had been seen as a middle-class, professional woman, she would not have received such cooperation. It was also helpful that she could speak Urdu and Punjabi. People trusted her with confidential information.

Her relationship with the teachers was different. The head made a point of not introducing her to the staff as a researcher. She implies that this may have been threatening to staff who may have acted artificially in front of her. She argues that teachers were less likely to think this way if they only thought of her as a Pakistani woman.

e This is a reasonably good response which makes its points well. It reflects what Bhatti says in Item A — note that the candidate puts words lifted directly from the text in Item A into inverted commas to acknowledge the source. However, the candidate does not use the item to full effect. A large amount of useful information is ignored, e.g. Bhatti's 'wife/mother persona' could have been explored in greater depth, as could her relationship with both the children and the teachers. This answer would score 6 out of a possible 10 marks.

(d) In order to collect quantitative data from African-Caribbean and Asian parents, I would probably use a survey questionnaire. This type of survey aims to collect large amounts of statistical data in a relatively short period of time from a large sample. The research design demands that this type of information be gathered from a representative sample scattered across four cities. A closed questionnaire is likely to be cheaper, quicker in gathering data and more manageable considering the geographical distances involved than conducting a series of interviews. The survey questionnaire would also allow me to gather a greater volume of data relating to parental attitudes.

e This is quite a good introduction. Many candidates fail to pick up marks because they choose research methods which are inappropriate. For example, choosing participant observation to investigate attitudes and motives is not recommended. The candidate chooses an appropriate method for collecting quantitative information and justifies the choice by outlining the aim of the method and linking this to the research context. The candidate also cites cost, time and geographical distance as factors influencing the choice of method. The final sentence is weak because it fails to explain why survey questionnaires gather a greater volume of data.

Another reason for choosing the survey questionnaire is that positivists praise its scientific reliability. All questions are standardised, meaning that it would not matter whether my sample is African-Caribbean or Asian, or where it is located, because all my respondents would be subjected to the same stimuli in the form of my questions about their attitudes towards education. The fact that each of my sample would receive a questionnaire rather than being interviewed should mean that my research would be reasonably objective and free from bias, especially if I had designed my questions to avoid the sort of problems normally associated with loaded, leading and ambiguous questions. Interviews could have led to various types of interview bias and effects, e.g. people might not have cooperated with my interviewers because they felt threatened by aspects of their character or status. Another sociologist could use the questionnaire to replicate my study in another part of the country with a similar sample and should get similar results.

e There is evidence so far that the candidate is focusing on the context. Candidates at this stage often deliver a list of strengths of a particular method without really thinking about how this relates to the research context. However, this candidate links knowledge of positivism, science, objectivity and reliability to the context throughout. Notice too how the candidate takes the opportunity to discuss why interviews would not be used, which by implication explains why questionnaires would be a better option for that context. However, the answer would have benefited from further detail in regard to 'loaded, leading and ambiguous questions' — this is a little vague and requires examples as illustration.

Access to an appropriate sample of African-Caribbean and Asian parents would require some careful thought. It should be fairly easy with the cooperation of the local education authority (LEA) to get a list of schools in London, Birmingham, Bradford and Leeds and to break these down into ethnic groups. Most LEAs are now required to collect this information. I would then select at random two schools in each area with at least 40% of their population from ethnic minority backgrounds. Once I had identified my schools, I would target parents' evenings in these schools and hand out my questionnaires to African-Caribbean and Asian parents attending these. Each questionnaire would have a covering letter attached which would explain my intentions and ask for their cooperation, assuring them of both their anonymity and confidentiality.

e This is an interesting way to go about gathering a sample. It is perfectly legitimate to assume that the LEA and schools in the area will cooperate with you because you are sponsored by a respected organisation, i.e. the Commission for Racial Equality. Similarly, the idea of going for schools which have 40% ethnic minority pupils is also a good one because this information is freely available. However, despite the excellent references to covering notes, the candidate's decision to distribute the questionnaires at parents' evenings is weak because the topic of the research is why African-Caribbean and Asian parents tend not to attend such meetings. In other words, the intended subjects of the research may never receive a questionnaire.

Next I would have to think about how to go about sampling my population. I would have a choice between random and non-random forms of sampling. Non-random forms allow all the people on the sampling frame an equal chance of being selected. This supposedly limits the possibility of bias creeping into the selection of the sample. The selection of the eight schools to be used across the four areas would be done randomly. However, in regard to choosing my final sample of African-Caribbean and Asian parents, I would use a non-random method of sampling. A sample of parents who attend parents' evenings is a form of quota sample and would give me insight into what motivates such parents to get involved. This would give me some ideas about why other ethnic minority parents don't get involved.

e The value of this paragraph lies in its constant contextualisation — the candidate focuses on the research proposal in the question and does not fall into the common habit of merely listing bits of knowledge without any reference to parents' attitudes. The discussion of sampling here is reasonably valid and demonstrates knowledge and understanding. Note too that the candidate attempts to explain the focus on parents attending parents' evenings. However, the candidate seems to be approaching the problem backwards. It seems unlikely that researching the parental attitudes of those who do attend parents' evenings will give insight into those who do not. Moreover, there is a lack of key concepts in this section. Discussions of sampling procedures require some reference to concepts like representativeness and generalisability. Note too that the candidate fails to recognise that categories such as 'Asian' are problematical in that this includes a range of different nationalities, religions, etc. which may impact on attitudes towards education and school activities.

I would also need to think about how to turn the research proposal into questions for my questionnaire. This is operationalisation and it would be necessary to make my research findings valid, i.e. that they would reflect the attitudes and feelings of the parents in my sample. I would therefore need to define terms like 'school activities'. Item B gives me some ideas in terms of parents' evenings, open days and parent–teacher association meetings but I would add other categories such as attendance at school prize days and sports days and visits to school art exhibitions in which their children might have displays. I would also need to

operationalise what I mean by 'involvement', e.g. for some people, this may mean frequency of visits whilst for others it may mean nature or length of visits. I would also need to think through how I intend to operationalise potential reasons for both involvement and non-involvement. For example, I would need to explore possible cultural reasons such as language and religion as well as potential practical factors such as family and work commitments. I would need to investigate attitudes towards education in general and the school and teachers in particular. It is likely that these possibilities would require a questionnaire made up of closed questions for factual information about people's social backgrounds and their children's relationship with the school. The questionnaire would also need open questions to allow respondents to explore their own interpretation of social reality rather than have it imposed on them by me.

e This is a useful section which demonstrates a clear understanding of what is meant by operationalisation. The candidate attempts to identify categories from which questions might be drawn. However, the answer would be improved by specific examples of questions accompanied by explanations of how each one operationalised the research question, i.e. why particular types of parents are reluctant to involve themselves in school activities. The reference to how the questionnaire would look in regard to closed and open response questions is a good one.

Overall, this is a reasonable response. The candidate demonstrates some knowledge and understanding of research methods and process as well as concepts such as reliability and validity. However, the weakness which undermines the whole response is the decision to distribute the questionnaires at parents' evenings, effectively excluding the most relevant research population. Although research into those parents who do get involved may yield some insight into parental attitudes, it is likely to be the case that parents who do not get involved have a completely different set of attitudes which would be missed by this research. However, the response does demonstrate a genuine attempt to get to grips with the research problem and context, and therefore deserves reward. The candidate would score 4 out of a possible 6 marks for knowledge and understanding and 5 out of a possible 8 marks for the evaluation of the method chosen, making a total of 9 marks out of 14.

(e) The first weakness that I can see would lie in my choice of method. Whilst the questionnaire is a scientific method, there are some sociologists who might argue that it would not be very effective in collecting information about the experiences, motives and attitudes of African-Caribbean and Asian parents. Interpretivist sociologists point out that the questionnaire is an artificial method that is likely to generate artificial rather than natural or valid data. This is because questionnaires interrupt the normal flow of social life and their appearance may be resented and resisted, e.g. through non-response. In addition, despite my open questions, I have defined the topic areas worth investigating by including particular questions. However, because I am not African-Caribbean or Asian or even a parent with children at school, I might not be aware of particular reasons why such parents do not involve themselves in school activities. Moreover, I could not be sure that the parents filling in my questionnaire would interpret my questions in the way I intended. The solution to this problem might be to carry out a series of unstructured interviews with a sub-sample of parents which would focus on identifying their concerns. These would then form the basis of my questionnaire.

e This is an excellent section which evaluates the use of the questionnaire from a theoretical perspective in a sophisticated way. It also offers a practical solution to the problems identified.

Another problem would result from my sampling process. I would assume that schools exist in these areas with an ethnic minority population of over 40%. However, ethnic minority children may attend a range of schools and consequently may not attend any one school in large numbers. I'm not convinced therefore that I would get a representative sample of both Asian and African-Caribbean parents. I might find that one group attended the parents' evenings more than the other. This would make it difficult to generalise to other African-Caribbean and Asian parents in the area. I could get over this problem by asking African-Caribbean or Asian children to take my questionnaire home, although the response rate might not be too good.

e This is not a successful section because it is still suffering from the same problem we saw in part (d), i.e. the intended sample is not appropriate in the context of the sociological problem being studied. However, the points made about representativeness and generalisability are fine. The suggested solution, ironically, might have been a better method of researching this topic than distributing questionnaires at parents' evenings.

Finally, one big problem might be my status as a white person. African-Caribbeans and Asians might feel threatened by my questionnaire. Most respondents to questionnaires demonstrate demand characteristics, i.e. they want to know what the motives of the researcher are, how the research findings will be used, whether the findings will be used against them, etc. They might therefore not be totally honest when they filled it in, undermining validity. I would also have to wait for them to fill it in and this, combined with a tiring evening talking with their children's teachers, might mean that they would not give my questionnaire, especially the open questions, enough attention. This might result in partial data which would tell me very little about their reasons for attending parents' evenings. The solution to this would probably be to ask them to take away the questionnaire and return it via their children, although this might affect my response rate negatively. I would also use triangulation — a variety of methods so that I could cross-check my findings from different methods.

e A valid and intelligent point is made about the possibility of researcher effect on parents. The point about demand characteristics is illustrated well. However, the point about parents filling in the questionnaires at parents' evening is again undermined by the inappropriateness of this sample being the central focus of the

research. In addition, the point about triangulation is wasted — the definition is weak and it is not clear what variety of research methods might be used and what cross-checking might take place.

Overall, this evaluation begins well with an emphasis on the interpretivist critique of questionnaires, making some good sociological points about researcher effect and demand characteristics. These points are always focused on the research context. It uses concepts like validity accurately, although the essential concepts, especially reliability, need to be developed further. The response is rather short (approximately 500 words) and the marks on offer suggest candidates should aim for at least 750 words in order to add depth to the response. In addition, the evaluation and solutions are undermined by the candidate's decision to focus on distributing questionnaires to those parents who attend parents' evenings rather than directly researching those who do not. The response becomes rather lazy towards the end, as exemplified by the vague references to triangulation. If you decide to discuss this concept, you must explain it in some depth and justify adopting it with examples of how it would work in practice. This candidate would therefore score only 8 marks out of a possible 14 for knowledge and understanding of the potential weaknesses of the research method. The response does address the research context but it is often in need of further development — it tends to lack depth and detail. It would score only 4 out of a possible 8 marks for evaluation, mainly because the solutions offered are basic and the use of concepts is disappointing. This candidate would therefore score 12 marks out of a possible 22.

Total mark: 37/60

Task

Examine parts (d) and (e) carefully and think about how you might rewrite the answers given so that they would gain higher marks.

Answer to question 1: grade-A candidate

(a) First, researchers who use a single method such as questionnaires or interviews often have to assume that their questions capture most of the motives and meanings behind social behaviour. However, observation, following a questionnaire or interview, can often supplement quantitative data because it can show up particular types of behaviour that the researcher had not thought about and consequently not included as a question in the original research.

Second, researchers may interpret raw data according to their sympathies with particular theoretical and ideological positions. Methodological pluralism allows the researcher to check his or her interpretation of the data against the first-hand accounts of those being studied, i.e. respondents can be asked whether the interpretation of the sociologist agrees with their view, so reducing potential bias.

e The candidate distinguishes clearly between two reasons. Both points are lifted skilfully from the data in the candidate's own words and demonstrate a perceptive understanding of methodological pluralism. The candidate would score the full 6 marks.

(b) First, it can be difficult to find samples and research teams committed to such long-term research. The sample may drop out, die, move away or simply refuse to cooperate any longer because they experience research fatigue. Consequently, the sample may start off as representative of a particular social group or as a cross-section of society but eventually refusals will mean that the sample will not be typical and data collected may not be generalisable to other similar social groups.

Second, if different researchers are used, it can be difficult for the research team to establish trust and rapport with members of the group being studied. Such bonds are essential if the research data are to continue to be characterised by high levels of validity. The '7-Up' Granada Television research into over 20 children, which has been conducted over 35 years since the sample was 7 years old, has been successful in terms of validity because the interview team has been led by the same individual over that period.

e The candidate identifies two problems successfully and explains and illustrates each using concepts such as representativeness, generalisability and validity. The answer would score the full 8 marks.

(c) Bhatti notes that the status of a researcher is an important factor to take into consideration when conducting sociological research. In particular, she notes that some of her statuses were very useful in establishing trust and cooperation with elements of her research population. Specifically, she was able to use her status as a young Pakistani bilingual woman to good effect. For example, she found that Asian parents trusted her because they could see that she had good relationships with their children. In addition, she found that her ability to speak Urdu and Punjabi resulted in Asian parents being willing to confide in her. She also used her status as a mother in her favour — Asian parents regarded her as trustworthy and non-threatening when she adopted a wife/mother persona. She argues that if she had been interpreted as a middle-class, professional, Asian academic, she would not have gathered such qualitative and valid data. The only group that seems to have kept its distance from her were teachers, who regarded her bilingual ability with suspicion, especially when she talked to disruptive children in Urdu and Punjabi. Data generated from teachers may therefore have been less valid than those obtained from parents and children.

e This detailed and in-depth summary gets to the heart of what Bhatti says about the effects of researcher status on the validity of research findings. The candidate also interprets all aspects of the data in Item A in his/her own words and would consequently be awarded the full 10 marks.

(d) I would use structured interviews to investigate the reasons why African-Caribbean and Asian parents in London and three other cities are reluctant to participate in school activities. I did consider using the survey questionnaire because this method

can gather large amounts of quantitative data in a relatively short period of time, but I decided against this because of the potentially high non-response rate, the impersonal nature of the questionnaire (which does not encourage any sense of trust and rapport) and the possibility that respondents might misinterpret questions. Instead, I would set up a trained team of African-Caribbean and bilingual Asian interviewers who would use an interview schedule. This would contain fixed pre-coded questions which aim to obtain factual information, as well as a series of attitudinal statements and ranking scales, e.g. 'I strongly agree', 'I strongly disagree' etc., which would hopefully uncover the reasons why parents do or do not involve themselves in school activities.

e This is an excellent introduction. The candidate chooses an appropriate method, i.e. structured interviews, and goes on to describe convincingly how the method would be organised in terms of the interview team and the variety of question-types planned. It is notable that the candidate is keeping an open mind concerning the sample's attitudes to school activities. There is also a sound rationale for why the alternative method of questionnaires has not been used.

I would need to think very carefully about how to gain access to a sample of African-Caribbean and Asian parents across the four cities. I presume that funding and time would not be problems because of my sponsorship by the Commission for Racial Equality (CRE). There are obviously dozens of schools in these cities — what I would have to ascertain is which contain the ethnic minority groups I am interested in. However, I do know that local education authorities keep records of the ethnic composition of schools and I can presume that these authorities would cooperate with an organisation like the CRE to provide me with a sampling frame of schools in the four cities. I would sample two schools from each city chosen at random from these lists and, with the cooperation of the head teachers in the schools, prepare a sampling frame of African-Caribbean and Asian pupils. I would use a stratified random sampling procedure to select 10 pupils, i.e. five African-Caribbeans and five Asians from each school, making 80 pupils in all.

e The candidate is thinking through methodological issues such as access, sampling frame and random sampling procedures. A mature comment is made with regard to funding, and the candidate's awareness of the status of the CRE is used effectively.

Random forms of sampling are important because if I were to use non-random methods such as quota sampling I might consciously or unconsciously only select those pupils that fit a particular profile, e.g. African-Caribbeans and Asians from middle-class backgrounds. Random sampling reduces the danger of such subjective bias. However, I do think it is important to stratify my sample further. 'Asian' is a catch-all term that disguises the cultural and religious diversity present among the Asian community in the UK. In some schools I might be able to set up sampling frames organised around Indian, Pakistani or Bangladeshi origins or religious affiliation, e.g. Muslim, Sikh or Hindu. This sample would probably be more representative of the Asian population of the four cities and might serve to give me further insight into attitudes towards education. Moreover, it would mean that I would be able to generalise from the data collected.

A good discussion of the practicalities of sampling is developed here. The candidate is aware of the problematical nature of terms like 'Asian' and makes a creditable attempt to stratify this group in order to access a range of cultures and religions. The concepts of representativeness and generalisability are used accurately.

Once I had finalised my sampling frames I would use a computer to select 10 pupils from two schools in each area at random. These pupils would be systematically selected from Year 7 and Year 11 lists, i.e. pupils who have just started their secondary education and those going into their GCSE year. These pupils would take home a letter addressed to parents outlining the research aims and asking for their cooperation in terms of being interviewed. Anonymity and confidentiality would be guaranteed in the letter. It would also be important that letters to Asian parents should be supplemented by the same letter in Punjabi, Urdu or other home language. Those parents who agreed to be interviewed would receive a home visit from one of the interview team soon after to explain the nature of the research and to arrange a time at which a more extensive interview might take place.

The candidate is rightly aware of the need to take each stage of the research in turn, despite the fine detail. Consequently, some thought has gone into how a sample might be persuaded to cooperate with a team conducting sociological research.

It would be extremely important for the people doing the interviews to be trained properly. I would use ethnic minority interviewers in order to minimise interviewer effect or bias. Hopefully, being interviewed by people sharing their ethnicity would generate some trust, rapport and cooperation, and produce valid data. My interviewing team would also be composed entirely of women. As Bhatti points out in Item A, women researchers are regarded as less threatening than male researchers. This is not to say that the interviewing would be successful. I would have to make sure that my interviewers were well trained and that they understood that their body language, facial expressions, etc. might undermine the interview process if not controlled. They should be trained to spot whether parents understand the questions and be willing to clarify their meaning. Finally, I would encourage my Asian interviewers to converse in the home language of the parents in order to make absolutely sure that language did not act as an obstacle to their understanding of the questions.

This is another perceptive passage which discusses intelligently how the status of interviewers may affect the validity of the research findings across a range of potential problems.

The design of my interview schedule would be crucial. Positivist sociologists are very keen on this method because of its scientific characteristics. For example, all parents in my sample should be exposed to the same stimuli in the form of standardised questions which follow the same logical sequence. This would mean

that my interview schedule would be reliable — if other sociologists were to adopt it and use it on similar samples in other parts of the country they should be able to cross-check and therefore verify my findings. In other words, differences between parents should indicate real differences in attitudes, especially if the questions I used were objective and did not reflect my personal opinions, prejudices, etc. Question design needs to be scientific, so I would need to avoid leading questions like 'Don't you think education is a good thing?'. Such questions force a certain type of response because people do not wish to be seen subscribing to 'bad' things. Similarly, loaded or emotional questions, e.g. 'Are you supportive of your children?', should be avoided because few people are going to admit to not being supportive. Hopefully my interview schedule would produce lots of statistical information which could be used to compare parental attitudes across cultural groups, cities, etc.

e This is another strong section which focuses on the theoretical rationale for choosing to use structured interviews.

Operationalisation would be a crucial stage in my research. I would need to somehow break down 'reasons for involvement or non-involvement in school activities' into questions or statements that could be assessed in terms of attitudinal scales. For example, I could ask questions which produce comparative statistical data in terms of frequency of visits to schools for specific occasions such as parents' evenings. Quantitative information can also be produced from attitudinal scales in that I could ask people whether they 'strongly agree', 'agree', 'disagree', 'strongly disagree' with a series of statements relating to involvement in their children's education. Examples of this could be 'Parents should liaise regularly with schools in regard to their children's education' or 'Schools do not do enough to establish relationships with parents' or 'My child's school does not take enough account of our religion'. As these examples show, operationalisation of 'involvement' would need to include not just parental involvement or non-involvement in schools but the schools' involvement or lack of it in the home background of the pupil. I would explore a range of home, cultural, religious and school-based factors which might affect involvement in school activities and which could be measured statistically using attitudinal scales.

e In this intelligent discussion of operationalisation the candidate examines how different types of question might measure aspects of 'involvement or non-involvement' in school activities.

Overall, this is a very strong response. The candidate demonstrates excellent knowledge and understanding of a research method, i.e. interviews, and the research process. In addition, the candidate applies this knowledge to the research context in a convincing fashion and would score the full 6 marks for knowledge and understanding. The choice of research method and the process is justified clearly and convincingly throughout, so the candidate would score the full 8 marks for evaluation. The candidate would therefore pick up all 14 marks available.

(e) There are a number of potential weaknesses of my planned research which might undermine the validity of my research findings. Firstly, interpretivist sociologists would point out that my choice of method might be problematic because standardised schedules like mine allow no freedom for the researcher to elaborate or make changes in response to something that the respondent might say that gives a fresh insight into what is being studied. In other words, probing for deeper meanings is prevented by the inflexible nature of the method. Moreover, the nature of the device would not allow the parents to really explain their experiences of school activities or the reasons why they do not participate in any significant depth or detail. Most importantly, there is a danger that my interview schedule might reflect only my interpretation of how parents behave in regard to making links with schools. In addition, my lack of experience as a parent and my inexperience of both African-Caribbean and Asian cultures may mean that the questions I would design and the fixed choices I would present to the parents may not resemble the experiences of parents. This might be off-putting for parents if they were to see little of their reality embodied in the questions. My questions might therefore alienate the parents and undermine both the reliability and representativeness of the study (i.e. by resulting in a high non-response rate) and its validity because the questions would only allow them partially to explore their experience. I would not get the full picture of how they feel.

e This is a good section which looks at problems of validity from a number of positions. In particular, there is a good evaluation of structured interviews from an interpretivist position.

There is a solution to these problems. A number of pilot unstructured interviews could be carried out which would allow a sub-sample of parents (white as well as members of ethnic minorities) to explore their perceptions of schools, teachers, etc. in depth. The data generated could form the basis of the standardised questions in my interview schedule. Most importantly, the questions would validly reflect parents' concerns rather than my limited experience.

e The candidate proposes an excellent solution which addresses the issue of validity.

Another problem with interviews is that they are time-consuming, meaning that my team and I could only conduct 80 interviews in all. This sample is obviously limited considering the number of ethnic minority parents with children in school. Although I had attempted to generate a representative sample, I would only choose 10 children per school. My stratified sampling frame may generate 40 African-Caribbean and 40 Asian parents but other variables which might affect reasons for involvement, e.g. social class, religion, etc., may be disproportionately represented. These question marks with regard to representativeness might undermine my ability to generalise to all ethnic minority parents. I might have to be happy with making observations about the involvement of ethnic minority parents in particular schools in London, Birmingham, Leeds and Bradford.

This is an intelligent commentary on representativeness and generalisability. The candidate understands that these concepts are not always achievable and that sociologists sometimes have to be content with making observations about particular groups within certain social contexts.

Some sociologists would take issue with me for using interviews. It is suggested that the reliability of this method and the validity of research findings generated by this method are open to question. Reliability is allegedly undermined by the fact that interviews are interaction situations involving unequal power relationships. In other words, they are difficult to replicate because the dynamics of any interaction are always different. Despite trying to standardise the interview experience by using ethnic minority female interviewers, I would never be sure that the interviewees were responding to the questions. They might instead be responding to the interviewer, e.g. by taking an instant dislike to them. In addition, the data collected by interviews might be partial or distorted because of demand characteristics (i.e. parents may feel threatened or criticised by the research or wonder how it might be used against them despite guarantees of anonymity and confidentiality), and parents might not be totally open and honest in their dealings with my interviewers. People might also protect their privacy or motives by engaging in yea-saying, i.e. saying they agree with things even if they do not, because they want to please the interviewer. Another problematic reaction, known as the social desirability effect, would arise if parents, in their desire to appear in a good light, avoided admitting to negative behaviour with regard to education. The only way around this problem would be to make sure that all interviewers were trained in recognising the symptoms of potential threats to validity. Cross-checking could also take place if other methods were adopted, e.g. two case studies of one Asian and one African-Caribbean family could be conducted in which detailed and in-depth data could be collected via unstructured interviews and diaries documenting contacts with the education system.

This is a thorough review of possible interviewer effect/bias which takes a multi-angled approach to the problem using a range of concepts such as demand characteristics, yea-saying and the social desirability effect. The solutions offered indicate a perceptive understanding of sociological research.

The design of my interview schedule would also be a potential minefield. Designing an objective questionnaire which does not reflect the ideological bias of the researcher is almost impossible. On top of this, I would need to avoid questions that are ambiguous, i.e. it would be crucial that questions were interpreted by all parents in the same way so that parents were responding to the same stimuli. I could not guarantee that this would happen. I would have to trust that all my interviewers were capable of delivering the questions in ways that wouldn't elicit invalid responses. I would also need to avoid questions that contained technical words or phrases that respondents might not understand, and vague words like 'generally' because these often mean different things to different people. The design of my interview schedule and a standardised delivery by my interviewers should ensure reliability, but I would never be sure that respondents were not turned off by the artificiality of my research device or what they interpreted as patronising or misdirected content in the form of the questions and fixed-choice responses.

The candidate demonstrates a good understanding of the potential problems of questionnaire design and how the technicalities of question writing might have a negative impact upon reliability and validity.

One way of gaining some forewarning of these potential weaknesses, and therefore avoiding both a poor response rate and data which do not reflect the real lives of the people I am studying, would be to conduct a series of pilot interviews to provide guidance on the clarity of my interview schedule and the effectiveness of my interviewers. This should give me an insight into potential non-response and refusals to cooperate, test the adequacy of my sampling frame and provide a critique of the sorts of issues included. For example, I might find that pilot study respondents complained that I had left crucial information out or that some questions were unnecessarily intrusive. A good researcher should be willing to respond to such criticism and modify the interview schedule accordingly in order to improve the validity of the data gathered.

The candidate is thinking through each stage of the research process, as seen in this solid review of the value of the pilot study.

Attitudinal scales might also create particular problems for me. I've already said that research subjects often want to please and engage in yea-saying. I might find that people agree rather than disagree when faced with attitudinal statements. People might also interpret commands like 'strongly' in different ways. They might have no opinion on an issue but feel obliged to give one. They also might feel strongly about aspects of schooling and school activities not included in my list of statements. Again, a pilot study should flag up these issues.

Pertinent and intelligent observations are made here about attitudinal questions.

Operationalisation would be a potential disaster zone because I might operationalise school activities and the experience of parents in a way that didn't capture the 'truth' of respondents' interaction with school. I might, of course, also operationalise the whole research problem in a qualitatively different way to other sociologists studying the same problem, especially those who have more in common with the ethnic character of the respondents. It would therefore be important that, in addition to the pilot studies, I established informal contacts with African-Caribbeans and Asians involved in the field of secondary education, whether as teachers, governors or members of parent–teacher associations, in order to gain insight into what meaning school and school activities have in particular communities. Such contacts should ensure greater validity at the operationalisation stage.

e The candidate demonstrates a perceptive understanding of the problems of meaning and interpretation that can undermine the process of operationalisation.

Overall, the candidate has focused on a range of relevant potential problems and demonstrated an insightful knowledge and understanding of theoretical and practical issues, using the key concepts of reliability and validity accurately. Moreover, the candidate shows a strong grasp of evaluative issues in regard to interview bias and interpretation and suggests workable solutions which are always focused on the research context. This response is about the same length as the response to question (d), despite more marks being available. However, the quality of the response is excellent and would generate full marks, i.e. 14 marks for knowledge and understanding, and 8 marks for evaluation, making 22 marks in all.

Total mark: 60/60

Question 2

Item A

The National Survey of Sexual Attitudes and Lifestyles conducted face-to-face interviews with 18,876 people from a randomly selected group of households across Great Britain about a wide range of sex-related issues. The table outlines the findings of the study in regard to the number of sexual partners people have during the course of their lifetime.

Number of partners	Men (% in each age-group)				Women (% in each age-group)			
	16–24	25–34	35–44	All	16–24	25–34	35–44	All
0	19·6	3·5	1·8	7·2	17·7	0·9	0·9	5·3
1	14·9	8·4	10·7	11·0	18·1	16·2	20·8	18·3
2	8·2	7·2	7·2	7·5	11·1	10·8	10·9	10·9
3–4	16·6	14·3	13·4	14·6	17·1	19·7	21·5	19·6
5–9	21·0	25·2	28·3	25·2	21·5	29·8	26·6	26·5
10+	19·7	41·4	38·7	34·6	14·6	22·7	19·4	19·4

50,010 addresses were originally selected from the Postcode Address File for inclusion in the sample. One major issue was the best way for the interviewers to introduce themselves to householders in order to maximise response rates. There was concern that people might refuse to take part because of the nature of the topic itself rather than because they were reluctant to participate in any survey. This would have had considerable implications for the representativeness of the sample. A great deal of thought therefore went into the initial moment of contact to ensure maximum cooperation. At each sampled household, the interviewer made an initial visit to provide residents with a set of briefing documents, explaining the purpose and rationale of the survey, and then called again to see if they were willing to participate. As a further measure to secure consent, it was made clear that potential respondents could choose to be interviewed by either a man or a woman, in case this was a factor affecting their decision whether or not to participate. About 31% of those initially contacted refused to take part but 63.3% of the initial sample completed interviews.

Sources: F. Devine and S. Heath, *Sociological Research Methods in Context* (Macmillan, 1999) and *The Lancet*, Vol. 358, No. 9296, December 2001.

question

(a) Using only Item A, identify *two* ways in which the researchers attempted to maximise response rates. (6 marks)

(b) Identify and explain *two* ethical problems that can undermine sociological research into sensitive subjects such as sexual behaviour. (8 marks)

(c) Summarise what the research findings in Item A tell us about sexual behaviour. (10 marks)

Item B

The Department of Health requires qualitative data about attitudes towards contraception held by teenagers aged 16–19 across different regions of the UK. You have been asked, as a sociological researcher, to design a proposal which will target a sample of teenagers who are currently in sexual relationships.

(d) Outline and explain the research process you would adopt in collecting qualitative data on teenage attitudes towards contraception. (14 marks)

(e) Assess the potential weaknesses of the research proposal, explaining briefly how you would intend to overcome them. (22 marks)

■ ■ ■

Answer to question 2: grade-C candidate

(a) Two ways in which the researchers attempted to maximise the response rates were that, first, they went to see the people that they wanted to interview and, second, they gave them the choice of whether to be interviewed by a man or a woman because they thought that it might make a difference as to whether people would participate or not.

e Some interpretive ability is displayed here, but it would benefit greatly from further explanation and illustration. Visiting potential interviewees is identified correctly, but the candidate fails to make clear how this would improve the research. The second point, about gender, is valid too, but the candidate does not spell out what difference this makes. This candidate would therefore only pick up 3 marks out of a possible 6.

(b) One ethical problem that could undermine sociological research on sensitive subjects is that sexual behaviour is very private to people and they may not want to discuss it with a stranger, although if the interview is in their home they may feel more relaxed. The problem is the way people might feel that the research is intruding into their personal lives. The second problem is that some people may be having sexual problems. If they started to talk about them with a researcher who then left, they might feel that they had been used and the researcher might even have psychologically damaged them by raising the issues in the first place.

e The first ethical problem is dealt with well. The candidate flags up issues of sensitivity, intrusion and privacy and even suggests a potential solution. The second ethical problem identified is also sophisticated, i.e. the notion that sociologists might take advantage of their subjects is an intelligent one. The candidate would score the full 8 marks for these observations.

(c) The findings are about the number of sexual partners that people have had in their life so far. The data are divided into males and females and then subdivided into three age-groups. The older people get, the more likely they are to have had a sexual partner — only 1.8% of males and 0.9% of females had had no sexual partner by the time they got to the 35–44 age-group. Women were more likely to have had a sexual partner by the age of 44 than men.

e This summary of findings identifies two trends in sexual behaviour accurately but misses out a lot of relevant trends, e.g. relating to monogamy and 'promiscuity'. This response, therefore, is far too short and lacks depth. It would gain only 5 of the 10 marks available.

(d) I have been asked to collect qualitative data from teenagers aged 16–19 across the UK who are in sexual relationships. My target population is all teenagers in sexual relationships. However, sexual relationships are very private so it would be unlikely that I would be able to find a sampling frame for selecting all teenagers in sexual relationships. I would contact the Family Planning Association in five large cities across England and Wales and ask if they would be willing to put out copies of a leaflet advertising my research interest (e.g. during young persons' drop-in sessions). This sort of non-random sample is known as 'opportunity sampling' because I would be accessing an agency which I know has contact with young people seeking contraception or advice about it.

e The candidate recognises the problems of collecting data of this type and correctly points out that no sampling frame exists which lists teenagers in sexual relationships. The idea to target Family Planning Association clinics is not a bad one and the candidate correctly identifies the sampling method as 'opportunity sampling'.

By doing the research in five cities I would get a representative sample of teenagers. I would give my name and address on the leaflet and ask them if they were between 16 and 19 and if they would be prepared to take part in the research. I would ask them to contact me if they were. I would hope that I would get about 5–10 replies from each session which would give me 50 people. I would then contact them and introduce myself on the phone and give some more information about the research. I would tell them that the research was being done for the Department of Health and that whatever they said would be treated anonymously and confidentially. I would also tell them that it was being done in a number of centres.

e The candidate decides to target five cities in response to Item B's focus on 'different regions of the UK'. However, the candidate's assumption that this would be 'representative' is not really explained — the answer needs to focus on the make-up of this sample. Is it going to be equally male or female? Is social class going

question

to be taken into account, etc? The reassurance of anonymity and confidentiality is good, but this section is let down by a certain vagueness of intent.

Once they had agreed to take part I would arrange a time to see them for an informal, unstructured interview. I would ask them whether they wanted to be interviewed at home or to meet somewhere else. I would do this because I would want to be sensitive to them and also because if their parents were around, even if not in the room, they might not speak so freely. I would hope that by doing informal/unstructured interviews I would get a real in-depth insight into their attitudes and that would mean that my research would be valid. The unstructured interview is the right sort of method to use for this type of research, although I would need to make sure that the people who took part trusted me.

e The candidate has at last identified the intended method. It is a suitable one in terms of obtaining qualitative data, but important issues with regard to collecting data from different regions, operationalising attitudes towards contraception and identifying key areas to explore with respondents in interviews are ignored. Some pertinent points are made with regard to helping respondents trust the research and therefore improving validity, but the candidate misses the opportunity to demonstrate knowledge and understanding of key issues involved in using unstructured interviews in this particular research context.

The fact that I have similar characteristics and status to them, i.e. I am a teenager aged between 16 and 19 and a student, should assist me in terms of interaction. The respondents and I would have similar levels of power and hopefully this would mean that they would cooperate with me. Unstructured interviews are very flexible in that I would be able to follow up any interesting comments or observations in depth rather than being restricted by a questionnaire.

e This section demonstrates some knowledge of interviews in terms of status and power relationships and the flexibility of unstructured interviews. However, these ideas could have engaged with the specific research context more. Overall, knowledge and understanding of unstructured interviews is satisfactory but disappointing when applied to the specific research context. It is important to remember that you will not be rewarded solely for your knowledge of particular methods. High-scoring candidates adapt knowledge of methods to the specific research situation identified by the item. This candidate would therefore score only 3 out of 6 marks for knowledge and understanding. Although the initial idea of using family planning clinics is a good one, it was neglected thereafter and the knowledge of unstructured interviews in the context of contraception use amongst sexually active teenagers was not developed. Similarly, the justification for using the methods selected remained basic. The candidate would therefore score only 4 out of a possible 8 marks for evaluation, making a total of 7 out of 14 marks for this response.

(e) I can see that there are a lot of weaknesses in my research proposal. Using only five cities would not really give me a good cross-section of the teenagers that I wanted to talk to so I would probably use three cities, one in the south, but not London because London is very different to other places and is not really representative, one in the North (Leeds) and one in Wales (Swansea). Then I would choose two other places which are more rural such as Devon and Cambridgeshire. I think that this would give me a better cross-section of teenagers and a more representative sample from which to make generalisations.

e The candidate is attempting to evaluate the choice of sample in regard to representativeness. This is only partially successful because it is unclear why these particular cities are being chosen. The rationale for the choice of rural areas is only implicit, i.e. they are to act as a source of contrast with the urban areas.

Another weakness is that I would only interview teenagers who go to the family planning clinics. The attitudes to sex of teenagers who don't go to those clinics, which might be seen as quite middle class, may be very different to those who do, so my research would be biased to the middle-class teenagers who are more aware of the importance of going to clinics for advice. To get access to other teenagers I could go to other places like youth centres or even schools and leave my leaflets in a prominent place. I may find that the response rate to my leaflets was very poor and I might therefore be forced to approach youth clubs directly in order to persuade teenagers to take part in my research.

e An interesting evaluation in regard to the type of teenagers who are likely to attend family planning clinics is made — the candidate is implicitly criticising the lack of representativeness of the potential sample. There is also an acknowledgement that the proposed research may have a problem with low response and a reasonable, although undeveloped, solution is proposed.

I would carry out informal interviews with my respondents, but that means the research would not be very reliable because they would be likely to tell me different things to what they would tell another researcher. The validity of the data I got would depend on the rapport that we managed to build up and the amount of trust between us. I think that I could distribute a short, structured questionnaire first so that some data could be checked by another researcher. That would make the research slightly more reliable. I think that doing unstructured interviews would give me good, valid data. If I built up a good relationship with the teenagers, it would give me an insight into their views, but because I would have found most of them from the family planning clinic there may be a greater number of girls. That would distort my research because as a girl myself I think that boys have a different attitude to sex than girls and my research could be biased. I could ask the girls who responded to my leaflet if they would ask their boyfriends whether I could talk to them as well.

e The first half of this section is reasonably strong — the candidate makes fairly good points about reliability and validity. The idea of cross-checking data is fine too, but deserves greater detail and development. The final idea about gender is pertinent, but is explained in a very long-winded fashion.

Interview bias is a major problem that I might face. I would have to be careful that respondents did not think I was being critical of their behaviour. I would have to make sure that my facial expression, body language and tone of voice remained neutral. I would not want them to think that I thought they were doing something immoral. There would also be the danger that they might think I was going to inform those in authority about their behaviour so I would need to constantly reassure them that the information would only be seen by me. In addition, another problem is that people often lie, exaggerate and misinform interviewers, especially when talking about deviant or sensitive topics. Finally, although I would be able to explore things I don't quite understand, there would always be the danger that I might misinterpret what my respondents say, especially when it came to analysing the large amounts of qualitative data collected.

e This is quite a good section which deals with several aspects of interview bias in a reasonably convincing way and demonstrates a good knowledge and understanding of the problems of interviews. It is a shame that apart from the point about morality, it is not focused on the research situation, i.e. sexual relationships/ contraception.

Overall, this response does display some knowledge and understanding of the potential weaknesses, although these needed to be tied more closely to the research context throughout the response. Unfortunately, the candidate does not find solutions to the problems identified. The score for knowledge and understanding would be 8 marks out of a possible 14. The evaluation of unstructured interviews was not bad — the final two paragraphs contain some good use of the concepts of reliability and validity. However, a failure to seek solutions undermines evaluation and consequently the candidate would score 5 marks out of a possible 8 marks for this skill, making 13 out of a possible 22 marks for this question.

Total mark: 36/60

Task

Examine parts (d) and (e) carefully and think about how you might rewrite the sections above so that they would gain higher marks.

■ ■ ■

Answer to question 2: grade-A candidate

(a) The first way in which researchers attempted to maximise response rates was to visit the chosen households in order to explain the aims and rationale behind the research. A further visit aimed to find out whether the household was willing to take part in the survey.

The second way was to assure respondents that they could be interviewed by either a man or a woman. This promise was motivated by the fact that talking about sexual behaviour is extremely personal and people are likely to feel more comfortable talking about their experiences and attitudes with a person of their own gender. Therefore, more valid data are likely to be generated.

e The candidate identifies two ways in which the researchers attempt to maximise response rates very clearly. Both ways are rationalised in an intelligent and convincing fashion. The candidate would be awarded the full 6 marks.

(b) Sensitive subjects such as sexual behaviour are difficult to research because the research might be perceived by respondents as prying into areas which are both intimate and private. They may feel reluctant to have their private lives aired for public consumption and will need to be convinced of the sociological value of such research. It is probably a good idea to reassure such potential respondents by guaranteeing both anonymity and confidentiality.

In addition, respondents may not wish to cooperate with this kind of research because they fear that their sexual behaviour may be judged negatively, especially if it relates to behaviours often regarded as immoral, such as promiscuity, homosexuality and adultery. For example, despite increased tolerance of homosexuality and decriminalisation, it is still difficult for people to come out as gay. Researchers need to convince respondents taking part in the research that the research is objective and does not involve making moral judgements about people's sexuality or behaviour.

e Two ethical reasons are identified and explained in detail. The candidate clearly understands the relationship between the need for sociologists to be ethical and sensitive sociological topics. This answer would score the full 8 marks.

(c) The data in Item A tell us that over one third of men claim to have had over 10 sexual partners during the course of their lifetime. Another quarter claim to have had between 5 and 9 sexual partners whilst only 7.2% of men claim virgin status. Unsurprisingly, the 16–24 age group is not as sexually experienced as the 25–34 age group or the 35–44 age group. 19.6% of men aged 16–24 claimed to be virgins whilst only 1.8% of those aged 35–44 claimed this status. However, the 25–34 age group claims more sexual partners than the 35–44 age group which tells us that sexual attitudes may have relaxed over the years. The figures for women tell a different sociological story. Both the 25–34 and 35–44 age groups are approximately 50% less likely than similarly aged males to have had over 10 sexual partners during their lifetime. This tells us that it is more acceptable in UK society for men to be sexually experienced compared with women. However, the sexual experience of women aged 16–24 is not dissimilar to men aged 16–24 across all categories of sexual partners. Interestingly, women on average are less likely than men to be virgins, i.e. only 0.9% of women are virgins at 25–44 years. Women are more likely than men to have had just one partner for life, i.e. they are more likely to be monogamous. Finally, the data tell us that the period 25–34 is the most sexually active period for both males and females.

This is a very detailed summary of the research findings which compares and contrasts the sexual behaviour of men and women and different age groups, and speculates intelligently on issues such as monogamy and changing sexual attitudes. It would be awarded the full 10 marks.

(d) I would use a social survey to collect qualitative data relating to attitudes. However, this would have to be approached carefully because the survey is normally used to collect quantitative data related to facts. Surveys use a combination of closed and open questions. I would use some pre-coded questions in order to collect some facts about my respondents, but the emphasis in my questionnaire would be on open questions. These would demand some work from the respondents in the sense that I would be asking them to write reasonably detailed answers to my questions. However, I would probably also use the Likert scale and ask people to indicate their strength of agreement with a particular statement or series of statements on a five-point range, e.g. 'strongly disagree', 'disagree', 'undecided', 'agree', 'strongly agree'. This latter strategy should help cut down the amount of writing respondents would have to do, which some might find off-putting. I could consider using different types of interview for this research, but the fact that the Department of Health requires data from across different regions of the UK would make this a more expensive and time-consuming proposal.

The candidate identifies a suitable method and clarifies how it would focus on qualitative data, i.e. through the use of both the Likert scale and open questions. A reasonable rationale for not using interviews is offered through the use of Item B.

As Devine and Heath note, research into topics like sexual behaviour and contraception face a problem in that people may refuse to take part because of the nature of the topic itself rather than because they don't like to take part in research generally. In other words, there are ethical problems facing research of this type. I would therefore have to be careful not to ignore the ethical guidelines laid down by the British Sociological Association for research of this type. I would need to guarantee the confidentiality of any information given to me and I should also assure my respondents of anonymity — they would not be identified when I came to write up my research.

The candidate shows an intelligent understanding of ethical issues and how they relate to this specific research context.

I think that both positivist and interpretivist sociologists would approve of my choice of research method. Positivists would approve of it because everybody in my sample should be exposed to the same stimuli in the form of the questionnaires. In addition, questionnaires are generally regarded as scientific because they are reliable, i.e. other sociologists can repeat them with similar samples and usually obtain similar results. They are also regarded by positivists as objective if care has been taken in terms of question design and sampling method. Finally, they result in quantitative information which can be compared and contrasted in order to reach decisions about the relationship between variables, i.e. cause and effect. My use of the Likert scale, for example, would hopefully help to quantify attitudes and beliefs about contraception.

e The candidate demonstrates a good knowledge of theoretical issues. These are not just listed but are related clearly to the research context.

On the other hand, I think interpretivist sociologists would also approve of my use of open questions. Interpretivist sociologists are generally concerned with collecting information relating to how people interpret the social world around them. They believe that the most valid data are those which come from the people actually being studied. The job of the sociological researcher is to make sure that the meanings people actually apply to the world around them are somehow conveyed in a true sense in sociological research. Therefore, to have the subjects of my research, i.e. young people in sexual relationships, respond in their own qualitative words would be approved of by interpretivists because it means I would be less likely to impose my definition of reality, i.e. my interpretation, on the data collected. I could also improve the validity of data further by making sure that I carried out initial pilot interviews with young people to collect qualitative data that could form the basis of my Likert statements.

e More relevant theoretical knowledge is demonstrated. The candidate clearly understands how the research process may reflect theoretical assumptions about how the social world is organised. The concept of validity is dealt with perceptively.

I would need to think very carefully about sampling. No sampling frame really exists of teenagers aged 16–19 who are currently in sexual relationships. In addition, whatever teenagers I used would need to be from different regions across the UK. I have considered getting the cooperation of family planning clinics and asking them to distribute my questionnaires to teenagers who ask them for free contraception. However, whilst this would gain me a sample of sexually active teenagers it would not guarantee me an unbiased sample. It is safe to assume that these teenagers have positive and educated attitudes towards contraception, since they see the need to visit a family planning clinic in the first place. Another possibility would be asking an editor of a magazine aimed at teenagers to include the questionnaire as part of a feature about teenage sex. Teenagers could be encouraged by the incentive of a prize (e.g. a free subscription to the magazine) to send back the questionnaires. Whilst this method would be likely to gain me a sample that is geographically dispersed across the country, again it would be problematic because I would prefer to obtain a sample of both males and females. There is no suitable magazine aimed specifically at males aged 16–19, although there are plenty of female ones. The sort of male magazine that I might use, e.g. *Men's Health* and *Loaded*, are aimed at men in their late teens and early twenties.

e This is an excellent discussion of the problems posed by the research proposal. As the candidate points out, no suitable sampling frame is available. There would also be the difficulty of finding a geographically dispersed group willing to take part in the research. The discussion regarding the possible use of family planning clinics

and teenage magazines demonstrates that the candidate has an excellent understanding of the process of research.

The nature of the research subject, the lack of an immediately accessible sampling frame and the request for data from different regions of the UK probably mean that I would not be able to use a random sampling method. I would have to think of a way of getting sexually active teenagers to volunteer to take part in my survey, and plan to obtain my volunteer sample by advertising on Radio 1. This is a subject of national importance and the sponsorship of the Department of Health should ensure that this network would take an interest in helping me recruit my sample. I could ask Radio 1 to advertise the survey intensively over a 2-week period. This would be supported by a poster campaign. Posters advertising the survey would be sent to schools and youth clubs across the country. I would ask them to put the posters up in sixth-form common rooms so that they coincided with the radio campaign. This would still leave me with the problem of getting the questionnaire to the sample. However, I could make the questionnaire available on the Radio 1 website and various other 'youth' websites. It might also be possible to persuade the Department of Health and the Family Planning Association to set up websites. Again, I would probably attempt to increase the response rate by offering some sort of incentive, e.g. all respondents would have their names put into a prize draw for a free tour of Radio 1. Once the questionnaire had been filled in, the respondent could click on an icon and e-mail it to me.

e This section indicates some very focused thinking on how to attract young people's participation in the research.

The operationalisation of this particular subject would need careful thought. I am primarily interested in 'attitudes towards contraception' held by 'teenagers currently in sexual relationships'. It seems to me that there may be differences in attitudes across different age groups despite the fact that the age-range is only 4 years. Males and females may also have different outlooks as far as contraception is concerned, e.g. it might be a good idea to explore who thinks about the need for contraception, who initiates its use within a relationship, whether there is a preference for different types, whether its use is regarded as positive or negative, and whether its use is aimed at preventing pregnancy, HIV or other STDs. It may be that the type of relationship has an impact on the use or non-use of contraception and attitudes towards it. I might therefore need to explore whether sexual relationships are casual or long term or whether those who engage in casual one-night stands have qualitatively different attitudes towards contraception compared with those who are in long-term serious relationships. There may be interesting contrasts to be made in the attitudes of different ethnic groups, different regions and even different ability groups.

e This is an excellent section. Candidates often neglect the crucial process of operationalisation. This answer demonstrates a good understanding of the sorts of question that might be asked in a survey of this type.

The questionnaire would therefore consist of two main sections. The first would deal with questions of a less personal nature, i.e. questions which would gain me factual information about age, gender, ethnicity, qualifications and area of residence. These questions would gradually merge into factual questions about the respondents' sexual experience. The second section would cover the more sensitive topic of how the respondents feel about contraception, how they interpret their sexual relationships in the context of contraception, what they feel about advertising campaigns, what they 'enjoy' or 'dislike' about current forms of contraception, etc. The ordering of questions would be absolutely crucial in terms of building up to the sensitive questions. If these came too early, the sample might regard the questionnaire as too intrusive and refuse to cooperate. I would also need to use language which respondents felt comfortable with. In particular, I would probably use the teenage vernacular for sexual activities so that the language of the questionnaire would be familiar to my sample. What is very important about all these questions is that they would be asked in a 'teenager-friendly' way and they would not be interpreted as being the product of authority, officialdom or moral guardians.

e This is a good overview of the questionnaire design — another area of research often ignored or neglected by candidates. Note too that there is further evidence in this section that the candidate is thinking about operationalisation issues and how these can be communicated effectively to the target group of teenagers.

Overall, the candidate demonstrates a commendable range of knowledge and understanding of both the research method and processes, such as sampling and operationalisation, necessary for investigating attitudes towards contraception amongst sexually active teenagers. In particular, the candidate focuses on the research context throughout the response, thus earning the full 6 marks for knowledge and understanding. The willingness to make sure that every decision is justified in detail means that this candidate would also score the full 8 marks for evaluation.

(e) Some sociologists would take issue with me for using a social survey to gather qualitative data about contraception from sexually active teenagers for a number of reasons. It can be argued that such a method does not have the strengths that unstructured interviews have in gathering data about attitudes, beliefs and feelings, especially about sensitive topics like sex. It is argued, mainly by interpretivist sociologists, that unstructured interviews are more suitable because they allow respondents to speak at length and in depth about particular topics without the constraints imposed by questionnaires which reflect the sociologist's view of what is important. Unstructured interviews give priority to the respondent's view of the world, and the data gathered are truly qualitative and valid because they are often presented in the respondents' own words with minimal sociological analysis. Surveys, on the other hand, depend on questionnaires which include questions and fixed responses which may be at odds with the experiences of respondents or which miss vital aspects because they are based on either the sociologist's interpretation of that world or on unrepresentative samples used as part of pilot surveys.

e The main strength of this section is its use of a theoretical base, i.e. interpretivism, to make some pertinent and perceptive observations about possible weaknesses in the research design. The candidate uses concepts such as validity extremely well.

I would attempt to overcome these problems by making sure that my pilot surveys used teenagers who were likely to be representative of the wider social group so that I could put together a questionnaire that was truly representative of their concerns. The reason I have decided that I would not use unstructured interviews is because I would need to collect qualitative data from different regions of the UK. Unstructured interviews, if they are to be conducted properly in an environment that encourages trust and rapport and therefore highly valid data, cannot be rushed. Surveys have the advantage of producing data a lot more quickly.

e The candidate focuses convincingly upon the use of pilot surveys as a solution to any possible questionnaire design problems and justifies the non-use of interviews.

Secondly, some positivist sociologists would object to my use of open questions and the Likert scale of attitudinal statements. They would probably question the reliability of my method in that there is a danger that different respondents may interpret these open questions in different ways and standardised responses are unlikely to be the outcome. There would also be the danger, despite the use of standardised Likert scales such as 'strongly agree', that respondents might not agree on what is actually meant by 'strongly'. Strength of feeling may differ considerably even among those who feel 'strongly'. There would also be the problems of yea-saying (people, on the whole, prefer to agree) and the social desirability effect (i.e. people prefer to please researchers and avoid difference, criticism and what they perceive as disapproval, especially in relation to subjects which have a moral dimension like sexual behaviour). These problems would be likely to undermine the reliability of my study and also the validity of my research findings. However, there would be little I could do to avoid such problems apart from constantly monitoring how my sample was responding and looking for trends which might indicate social desirability effects, especially at the pilot survey stage.

e This section shows an excellent grasp of theoretical issues. The concept of reliability is dealt with perceptively too. Excellent material is included on aspects of interview bias, indicating a strong knowledge and understanding of method and, most importantly, how it impacts on this particular research context.

One of the major problems I might have would be the subject matter of my research, i.e. teenage sexual relationships and contraception may be regarded as too sensitive and personal for a questionnaire. Teenagers might not cooperate with an impersonal questionnaire asking them about aspects of their intimate lives or they might feel threatened by such an issue because they are not sure how the information they give might be used. They may feel that admitting to sexual behaviour or sex without contraception would leave them open to criticism or moral disapproval, and consequently they may only give a partial or false account of how they behave and feel in order to avoid what they see as negative moral judgements being made about them. This is why it would be important to adopt good ethical practice. I would need to make clear my intentions right from the beginning by having a clear statement of my aims, and guarantee that the research was non-judgemental, that any information given would be treated with utmost confidentiality and that volunteers would not have to give names and addresses.

e This section focuses on the problems raised by the actual subject matter of the research proposal. The candidate demonstrates a strong understanding of the ethical dimension of the research process.

It is likely that my guarantee of anonymity would create further problems because I would be unable to follow up interesting data or cross-check accuracy or the authenticity of the source. I would have to trust that the questionnaire on the Radio 1 website would be filled in only by the age group that I wish to take part in the survey. This part of my research proposal would probably be the most unsatisfactory aspect. I couldn't guarantee that my sample was representative of sexually active 16–19 year olds. It might be that people who are not sexually active, especially young males, would fill in the questionnaire as a means of 'showing off' their masculinity. The fact is that anybody would be able to fill in this questionnaire. The only way around this problem would be to cross-check the validity of the Radio 1 responses by having a number of teenage focus groups who could examine examples of evidence gathered from the Radio 1 source and comment upon the reliability and validity of the data.

e The candidate has not been carried away by the idea of obtaining a sample through a Radio 1 campaign. This section shows a clear awareness of the pitfalls of such an approach. The solution offered, i.e. focus groups, is an interesting one, although it deserves a little bit more attention and detail.

Another problem relating to the data would be having no idea how many responses I might receive. It might range from dozens, which would limit my ability to generalise, to thousands — which would add strength to my ability to generalise. With a national radio and poster campaign behind my research I would hope to attract hundreds or thousands of responses. However, this would pose the problem of how to deal with the quantity of data received. The quantitative data should not be a problem if they are pre-coded — a computer program should deal effectively with them. However, a large volume of qualitative data might prove to be a problem and would probably require me to be selective, incurring the risk of over-emphasising findings which support particular political or ideological positions and being accused of bias. It might be impossible because of the sheer volume of qualitative data to use it all, but I would have to ensure that all points of view expressed by respondents were equally and objectively represented.

e Excellent evaluative skills are demonstrated in this section relating to response rate, representativeness, generalisability and bias.

My operationalisation of the subject matter, i.e. attitudes towards contraception held by teenagers currently in sexual relationships, would focus mainly on heterosexual relationships. I would therefore be guilty of making value judgements about sex which reflect the heterosexual dominance of our society. In other words, I really ought to include questions which allow people practising homosexual sex to take part. However, the age of consent for homosexual sex is 18 at this point in time and my survey could be accused of being ethically unsound because it could be seen to be condoning behaviour which is illegal for those aged between 16 and 17. Another idea to improve the quality of the data, especially their comparative value, would be to compare the views of males and females in the same sexual relationship towards contraception. However, the sampling process that I would adopt means that this would be impossible, though it might form the basis of any follow-up research using unstructured interviews, for example.

e The point about homosexuality is perceptive and the candidate shows sound awareness of another ethical dimension of sociological research.

Overall, this response shows that the candidate has a strong grasp of the potential weaknesses of the chosen research method and aspects of the research process, especially sampling and operationalisation. The answer demonstrates an excellent range of knowledge and understanding which is always focused on the research context, and the means of overcoming these problems is always stated in a way that directly addresses the research context. Theoretical issues related to design are also dealt with perceptively. Conceptual issues such as reliability, validity, representativeness, generalisability and ethics are addressed explicitly and accurately. You may have noticed that this response is not as long as the response to part (d). This is not a problem because the quality of the response is excellent — it is very focused on addressing the research context. This candidate would score the full 14 marks for knowledge and understanding and the full 8 marks for evaluation, making 22 marks in all.

Total mark: 60/60

Question 3

Item A

Qualitative methods were used to conduct the study. I spent 9 months as a part-time participant observer in primarily 'public spaces': at punk concerts, on the street, and at the rehearsals of a hardcore punk band. I wrote detailed notes as soon as possible after (and occasionally during) each session in the field. I also conducted nine semi-structured interviews with punk informants, knowledgeable and committed insiders who were not necessarily representative of the subculture as a whole, but who could provide me with detailed information about the subculture and its members. The interviews were tape-recorded and later transcribed. The informants ranged in age from 18 to 27, and were involved in punk at different periods of historical time. I attempted to choose informants who were beginning to become involved in punk, who were currently very involved, and who were no longer involved at all.

From the very beginning of the research, defining 'punk' was problematic. One of the first findings was that some individuals identified themselves as being punk but did not act or dress according to the punk ideal type, while other individuals who participated in the style and behaviours typical of the ideal did not identify themselves as punks. Punks, therefore, had varying identity standards, i.e. the punks in my study held different definitions or 'sets of meanings' for 'being punk'.

In my analysis, punks go through three stages in their punk careers, as seen in the table below:

Self-label as a punk	**Stage 1: Rebellion**	**Stage 2: Belonging**	**Stage 3: Belief in core values**
Definition of a 'punk'	Unconventional and non-conformist	Membership of a subculture	Belief in punk values more important than dress, looks, etc.
Behaviour	Anarchic: dress and hairstyle aims to shock and offend; being deviant	Conform to common standards of dress, behaviour and piercing	Individual 'do it yourself' creative expression
Core values	Rejecting and opposing mainstream values	Acceptance by peers for being a true punk, not a poseur	Personal integrity, individualism, honesty, being unique

I found that people who defined themselves as punk saw punk as a politically meaningful social movement when they were involved in it. However, they also argued that the movement had declined because punk had become fashionable or trendy. All my respondents said this had happened after they had become involved, regardless

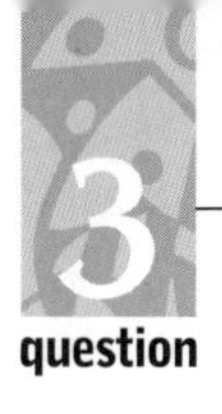

of when that involvement took place within the history of the subculture. Lester, for example, said: 'It was all about people that didn't have jobs; no prospects in life. Or they did have opportunities but they could see that careers and all that middle-class stuff was rubbish. But it seemed like around my second year of college (1984), there were all these little kids around 15 and 16 years old that were getting into punk because they were rebelling against their parents and not because they wanted to change anything.'

Source: 'Growing up Punk: meaning and commitment careers in a contemporary youth culture' by L. Andes, in (J. Epstein (ed)) *Youth Culture: Identity in a Postmodern World* (Blackwell, 1998).

(a) Using only Item A, identify *two* problems the researcher had when operationalising the meaning of 'punk'. (6 marks)

(b) Identify and explain *two* reasons why some sociologists prefer qualitative methods. (8 marks)

(c) Summarise what the research findings in Item A tell us about belonging to punk subculture. (10 marks)

Item B

The *Observer* magazine requires qualitative data about the social meanings that clubbers attach to dance music. You have been asked, as a sociological researcher, to design a proposal which will target a sample of male and female clubbers from a diverse range of socioeconomic and ethnic backgrounds.

(d) Outline and explain the research process you would adopt in collecting qualitative data on the social meanings that clubbers attach to dance music. (14 marks)

(e) Assess the potential weaknesses of the research proposal, briefly explaining how you intend to overcome them. (22 marks)

Task

This question is for you to try yourself. You should spend some time researching suitable material and making notes, and then try to write the answer in 90 minutes — the time you will be allowed in the examination. Below are a few pointers to help you get on the right track.

(a) Read through Item A at least twice before attempting the question. Note that the question clearly states 'Item A only', meaning that the bulk of your answer needs to be taken from the text in Item A (although you should put this in your own words). If you can think of something extra to make the problem clearer, that's fine, but don't get carried away. Finally, make sure you distinguish between the two problems by writing two brief paragraphs.

(b) The answer to this question is not in Item A. However, your revision should have informed you that it is interpretivist sociologists who prefer qualitative methods and data. Thinking through the strengths of unstructured interviews and observation will help you come up with two reasonably detailed reasons with illustrative examples. Again, make sure you distinguish between your two reasons by constructing two paragraphs.

(c) Look at both the textual data and the material in the table. Candidates often make the mistake of only using one aspect of the source. The whole of Item A needs to be looked at. Make sure you have a clear understanding of the table before you attempt to summarise what it is saying. In this case, the first column tells us how punks see themselves in terms of defining what a punk is, behaviour and values. The rest of the table tells us that being a punk involves three stages with different attitudes in each towards how punk is defined, behaviour and value systems.

(d) You have three main things to consider here.

- You need to find a suitable method for collecting 'qualitative data'.
- You need to think about how you would access or sample clubbers. Your sample must have an equal number of males and females and come from a diverse range of socioeconomic and ethnic backgrounds.
- You need to decide how you would operationalise the 'social meanings' associated with dance music, i.e. how it impacts upon the lives of those involved in it.

All of these factors, as well as appropriate theoretical and ethical issues, must be addressed as part of the research context if your response is going to get into the top bands of the marking scheme. Remember to use concepts such as reliability, validity, representativeness and generalisability throughout your response, whenever they are relevant.

(e) The best advice here is to deal with potential weaknesses and your proposed solutions using the organisation of part (d). In other words, if you have dealt with issues of sampling, access, representativeness and generalisability first in part (d), you should deal with the potential weaknesses of these first in part (e). Part (e) should therefore mirror part (d). Spend some time on solutions — candidates often let themselves down by not giving enough detail or by failing to illustrate their ideas. Triangulation, in particular, often suffers from this problem. It is not enough to say 'I intend to use triangulation' — you must justify this intention in some detail. Finally, be aware that accurate use of concepts like reliability and validity will be rewarded.

Personal Study

This section of the guide looks at how to approach the **Personal Study (2538)**. It examines how you need to present your ideas and findings in a way which will maximise the marks you achieve. In each case there are examples of excellent responses (grade A) and good responses (grade C). These take the form of extracts from the three major sections of the Personal Study: the Rationale, Research and Evaluation sections. Remember that the grade-A examples are not 'model' or perfect extracts — you need to develop your own 'final text', and this must reflect the specific focus of your research. The extracts just provide *one* way of achieving high marks, although you also need to realise that they do connect effectively with the bullet points on pp. 12–18 under the 'Personal Study guidance' heading, and this means that they automatically deliver all of the examinable skills at the highest level. If you want a grade A for coursework, you need to connect with these crucial bullet points too. The grade-C extracts deliver some of the all-important bullet points, but less effectively, or less fully. Students who achieve a grade C are doing most of the right things, but might be making particular mistakes or missing key points.

Examiner's comments

The extracts are accompanied by examiner's comments. These are preceded by the icon *e* and indicate where credit is due. For the grade-A extracts, the examiner shows you what it is that enables the candidates to score so highly. Particular attention is given to the use of examinable skills, outlined on pp. 12–18 under the heading 'Personal Study guidance'. For grade-C extracts, the examiner points out areas for improvement, specific problems and common errors. You might consider rewriting these extracts in a way which would gain higher marks.

Personal Study extracts

The Rationale section

Grade-A candidate

My research topic was gender and education and I eventually narrowed this down to the following research question:

'Is the post-16 curriculum gendered? — A questionnaire survey of aspects of male and female course choice in a NW London comprehensive.'

My research aims are to answer the following questions:

(1) Are there distinct differences in the courses/subjects chosen by males and females in my school sixth form? (I concentrated on AS and A2 courses.)
(2) If so, do these differences follow 'traditional masculine and feminine' subject lines?
(3) What factors motivate male and female students to select the courses they do?

My research objectives are to:

(1) Construct a questionnaire which will enable me to research my chosen area.
(2) Select a valid sample from an appropriate sampling frame.
(3) Administer my questionnaire effectively as a pilot study.
(4) Process my findings with my research question and aims in mind.
(5) Evaluate the whole research process.

e This is an excellent start. The candidate has obviously thought long and hard about all three issues raised above: research question, aims and objectives. Note that the two-part research question is crisp and informative, specifying the age-range involved, the method to be employed, and aspects of the sample (by sex and region). Look at how well the aims break the research question down into smaller issues for study. The objectives are concrete and achievable. If they are achieved, the student will be able to deliver the aims and thereby answer the research question.

My overall strategy was to use secondary data in the form of related studies and statistics to help me identify the issues I needed to ask questions about, i.e. to obtain ideas to build my questionnaire items around. Particularly useful in this respect were recent annual figures from the Department for Education and Skills and the studies done by Sue Sharpe (*Just Like a Girl*, 1976, 2nd edn 1994). As regards primary research, I carried out a direct questionnaire survey on a sample of 20 students from my school sixth form (my sampling frame) on a single day in February 2002. My sample was a systematic random sample, with tutors from 10 A-level tutor groups being asked to select one male and one female from their registers. The respondents had to be the fourth male and the fourth female on the register. Each respondent was then allowed time in tutor-period to complete the questionnaire. The tutors then collected the completed questionnaires and returned them to me.

I chose questionnaires as my method because I wanted to encourage honest, and therefore probably more valid, responses from my respondents. As I know many of the respondents personally, the alternative method which might have been used, interviews, could have led to respondents just telling me what they believed I wanted to hear. Using questionnaires avoids this problem, as it gives respondents anonymity, and they can therefore answer more thoughtfully and truthfully. Equally, using questionnaires is a much more time-efficient method compared to interviews. The latter, especially with semi-structured items, can take a long time to administer. My questionnaire had a mixture of open and fixed-response items, 12 items in all, so did not take too long to complete. Most important, though, was the fact that questionnaires, when used in the context I was using them in, tend to have a high degree of reliability — all of the respondents are answering the same questions, in relatively controlled and very similar circumstances. The research can be seen to be done in a reliable and scientific way. The evidence gathered will therefore be reliable, too.

Before administering the questionnaire I 'trialled' it with a male and a female sixth former, neither of whom would be in the final sample. They suggested a small number of changes to two different items, once they had completed their responses. The rest of the questionnaire seemed to work very well. I built their suggestions into the final research device.

e This is another strong section. What is striking is the amount of technical detail given, and the number of methodological concepts used effectively. There are also brief and appropriate references to secondary sources, sample composition, sample size and sampling technique. The candidate justifies the method used, says why an alternative method was considered less appropriate, and gives a range of practical details. In addition, the candidate refers to both validity and reliability — central issues in sociological research.

I chose this topic because a lot of research suggests that the education system has become more meritocratic, at least as far as gender goes, with girls now doing at least as well as boys in many subjects. I wanted to find out if gender socialisation and other factors were responsible for one remaining aspect of gender inequality and difference — subject choice.

e This final section reveals a good justification for the topic, and a thoughtful researcher's mind at work. The candidate has clearly located this research into gender and education within the broader context of research on the topic.

Grade-C candidate

'Gender and education — what do sixth formers study?'

Above is the title for my Personal Study and I carried out a survey to find out:
- whether some subjects are more likely to be studied by boys than girls (and vice versa)
- why people study the subjects they do

In order to obtain evidence for my study I intend to:

- carry out a questionnaire in my sixth form
- read related studies to see what they found
- analyse, conclude and evaluate my data

e A reasonable start is made by this candidate, providing a clear, two-part research question, plus aims and objectives, though these are not identified explicitly. The research question has been broken down into smaller questions to be answered, and the three objectives stated cover many of the tasks that need to be carried out. If you compare the above with the equivalent piece of writing for the grade-A candidate, though, you will see lots of differences. The research question above does not give as much detail to the examiner about method and sample as the earlier one does. In addition, the grade-A candidate gives detailed aims and objectives and often does so by using methodological concepts confidently and appropriately. Overall, the grade-A candidate reveals a deeper knowledge and understanding of research issues and the topic being studied.

My strategy was to distribute 18 questionnaires to sixth-formers at my school. They were selected from three different tutor groups, selected at random from all of the tutor groups in the sixth form. The Head of Sixth helped me to do this. I then selected, totally at random and from register lists, three girls and three boys from each group to be my sample. All of the groups are mixed as regards the subjects the students take, so this should work. I then gave the questionnaires to the students, together with an envelope with my tutor's name on it, to be returned to me via him.

I chose questionnaires because they are reliable (compared to interviews) and they also allow you to gather large amounts of quantitative data which can then be put into graphs, so you can see trends. They also allow anonymity for your respondents.

A study I was particularly interested in was Sue Sharpe's *Just Like A Girl,* carried out in the 1970s, which found that the girls she studied sometimes valued marriage and family life more than they valued education and career. Sharpe then repeated her study in the 1990s and found that girls had become much more education-minded and career-minded. I wanted to see if things had changed in my sample.

e At first glance there may seem to be a lot of similarities between the above and the equivalent piece from the grade-A candidate, but on closer examination there are many differences. The candidate outlines the strategy used, but gives no details about the questionnaire (types of items, number of items, etc.) and could have used more methodological concepts. Reference is made to a related study, but not in a way the examiner can give marks for. Many students think that topic knowledge will gain marks for them, but it is methodological knowledge that really counts. In addition, when justifying the method selected, the candidate does so in a generalised way. What the examiner really wants to see is the reason why a particular method is most valid for the study in question. Finally, the candidate gives no evidence of trialling the research device. There are a number of good features here, but there is plenty of room for improvement.

I chose this topic because there have been a lot of studies about girls doing better than boys in exams over recent years, and a lot of sociologists have discussed this. I found this topic interesting when we did it in class, but I thought that one area where differences between males and females probably still existed was in the subjects they opted for.

e The selection of topic is justified in much the same way by this candidate as by the grade-A candidate, again referring to a possible gap in the sociological literature that this candidate hopes to explore. The grade-A candidate's version is more clearly expressed and is conceptually more impressive, but this candidate has done quite well.

The Research section

Grade-A candidate

As I outlined in my Rationale, my questionnaire survey with 20 respondents involved the gathering of both quantitative and qualitative data through the application of open and fixed-response items. This meant that my study had both interpretive and positivist elements to it. However, it was intended to be a pilot-scale study, so the sample size was limited and this meant that any findings would be limited in terms both of their representativeness and my ability to generalise from them.

I took great care to operationalise key concepts in my study. Above all this meant that when I thought about the notion of a 'gendered curriculum', I had to consider all of the possible ways in which this might be happening in sixth forms. I then had to devise questionnaire items which would enable me to measure whether, and to what degree, this 'gendering' was going on. Put another way, I had to come up with a questionnaire which gave my respondents the chance to think about 'gendering of the curriculum' in the sixth form in all of the forms it might possibly take — for example, peer-group effect, teacher expectations, teacher role-models, etc. For the purpose of this study I have taken this central notion to mean 'the beliefs and expectations that some subjects are more appropriate for males, and some for females, and the processes that reinforce these beliefs and expectations'.

I had no significant problems about gaining access to a sample. I talked to the Head of Sixth Form and she suggested that I send a letter out in the sixth form registers a week before the date when I was due to distribute the questionnaires. This was to inform tutors and students and to ask for their cooperation. In the event, I got a 100% response rate, and the completion rate was also high, with most items being filled in effectively by each respondent. No ethical issues arose, though I naturally guaranteed the anonymity of my respondents (their names were not asked for) and the confidentiality of the data gathered. All respondents had the right to withdraw from the research, though none decided to do so.

e The candidate opens this section with another detailed and well-informed introduction. An impressive set of further details about the research strategy prepares the way for the presentation of the findings. The candidate makes a theoretical point before moving on to discuss representativeness and generalisability in a concise style. Operationalisation is discussed in a thoughtful manner. This piece of writing ends by dealing with the issues of access and ethics, briefly mentioning response rate and completion rate too.

Note: at this point candidates need to select which data they want to present to the examiner. It is not necessary to report on all of your findings. If a questionnaire has been used, then you will probably want to present, analyse and interpret only the data from the most revealing items, i.e. those which have generated the most useful information. For example, if you have already told the examiner that your sample had a 50/50 split of male and female, there is no need to report the data from the questionnaire item which recorded the sex of the respondents. Instead, you need to concentrate on the findings which link up with the research question and the aims of the Personal Study.

Questionnaire findings

Item 1 recorded the sex of each respondent.

Item 2 *'Please record clearly in the grid below the subjects you are studying/will study during your two years in the sixth form.'* (See Appendix for copy of questionnaire and grid.)

The responses to this question revealed some interesting patterns. I processed the responses under three subject-group categories: sciences, humanities/creative, and social sciences. I was able to put most subjects under one of the headings quite easily.

Seventy per cent of female students were studying either two or more humanities subjects, compared to only 15% of males. In contrast, just under 70% of males were studying two or more sciences, but less than 10% of females.

As regards the social sciences, the picture was more mixed, with boys and girls more evenly matched. Around 45% of both boys and girls were studying two or more social sciences.

Within the sciences, Biology was the subject opted for most of all by girls, and Chemistry by boys. Within the social sciences, Economics was very popular with boys, and Psychology with girls. Within the humanities/creative category, French was very popular with girls and English Literature with boys.

At this very early stage of analysis, and with the support of just the main findings from Item 3, it does appear that gender patterns are emerging. In purely quantitative terms, what our culture sees as traditional 'male' and 'female' subjects do seem to exist in my school. My first and second aims have been met by this data, with gender differences and some gender stereotyping of subjects being shown.

e The process of presenting, analysing and interpreting the data collected gets off to a good start. This candidate has given a heading, written out the item where appropriate, and

drawn out the key patterns observed. (A 'clean' and a completed questionnaire would be included in the Appendix, showing the way the data were recorded and giving an examiner an opportunity to examine the quality of the research device.) The candidate has made a cautious interim (or early) conclusion about how these patterns link up with the research question and aims. This commentary is just what the examiner wants.

Item 3 *'Please outline the central reason why you chose to study the subjects currently on your timetable.'*
The vast majority of respondents (60%) stated that 'career intention' was the main reason for selecting their subjects. This was followed by 'because I did them at GCSE and enjoyed them' (20%) and 'because I intend to study one of them at university' (15%). My respondents made no references at all to gender issues, but this might be what sociologists call 'false consciousness'.

e This is a concise summary of findings, together with some interpretation through the use of a valid sociological concept.

Item 4 *'How do you respond to the notion that males are naturally better at some subjects than females, and that females are better at other subjects?'*
This item, I thought, would cause a lot of controversy. I included it out of interest, but also because it would get my respondents thinking about issues that later items would deal with. Surprisingly, though, the majority of both male and female respondents agreed on this matter.

'In my experience, if you have a good teacher in a subject, it does not matter if you are a boy or a girl.'

'The media has a lot to answer for...they shape our attitudes a lot and that means giving us ideas about the sort of subjects each gender should be studying.'

The above quotes are representative of most of the comments I received. They stressed the 'nurture' rather than the 'nature' explanation of subject-choice. A few of my (male) respondents produced the odd sexist comment, but there were not many of these. There were also some comments from students who had obviously studied this topic in their psychology lessons, and they put forward theories to show that there were genetic differences. Overall, though, the data gathered revealed a disagreement with the idea in the item.

e This is another good demonstration of reporting and analysis. The candidate produces qualitative data by using selected quotes. Many students feel tempted to produce graphs or pie-charts, but a good quote can make an important point much more effectively. In addition, the candidate has again used key sociological concepts (nature/nurture) to make an analytical point.

Item 5 *'Is there a subject you would definitely not choose to study because it has a particularly "masculine" image which, as a female, you would not feel comfortable with? If you are male, is there a "feminine" subject you would never choose?'*

The responses to this item were quite mixed. Most respondents commented that social attitudes had changed and that 'barriers were breaking down', as one person said. Consequently, they did not feel they could say 'yes' to the question. One male, though, said that he would never consider doing beauty courses or childcare courses if they were offered at A-level. Another said that modern languages had a 'slightly female' image in his view. One female thought that 'technology-based courses', as she put it, were 'more masculine than feminine'. So, it is rather difficult for me to conclude with this set of data, because it is so mixed, but the respondents' perceptions of subjects seems to be that they have become less gendered.

The candidate deserves praise for the tone of this commentary. It is cautious but perceptive. It uses short quotes to very good effect, and ends by hinting that perceptions are not necessarily the same thing as reality.

Item 6 *'Can you think of ways in which the media might shape male and female attitudes to school subjects, perhaps with regard to depictions of males and females in certain careers? If so, please give brief details.'*
This item was very useful because it generated a lot of data. The material was usually about characters in soap operas, and the general view was that jobs for men and women in soaps were pretty much stereotyped. A couple of (female) respondents also talked about the way that women were still doing most of the housework and child-care in soaps, and they put forward the strong view that girls' attitudes to school subjects would be affected by such images — 'not many new men in Eastenders!' commented one of these respondents. The comments obviously talk about processes that link up with my second aim.

In this further passage of careful commentary the candidate gives an overview of a range of responses, rather than repeating very similar quotes. A link is also made with one of the research aims.

The candidate went on to ask questions about the role of peers, family, careers advisers and teachers in terms of the gendering of the curriculum. As above, the findings were processed systematically and thoroughly, with the central research question and research aims in mind. None of the items on the questionnaire 'drifted' from the main focus, so all the data were relevant and valid. Having processed all of the data, the candidate was able to respond to all three of the research aims and also to conclude firmly that the post-16 curriculum was indeed gendered in the sixth form studied, thus answering the research question directly.

Grade-C candidate

I distributed a questionnaire which had 10 items. I operationalised 'gender' in my research as meaning 'socially acceptable behaviour for the two sexes'. For the purpose of this study, by 'education' I mean 'studying in the sixth form'. I operationalised these concepts in my questionnaire. All of the questionnaires were completed within the same week. I achieved a 90% response rate (approx.).

Findings

Item 1 *'Are you male or female?'*
My sample was split, half boys, half girls.

Item 2 *'Please list the subjects you are studying in the sixth form.'*
When I analysed the replies I found that there was some gender bias. Out of 16 respondents, I found that modern languages and physics were the subjects most clearly linked to either female or male students. (A discussion with my Head of Sixth confirmed that this was the general picture.) Other interesting patterns were also clear. Sciences were more 'masculine' than 'feminine'. Arts subjects were more mixed, with a less clear distinction than in sciences. The health and social care course was very 'feminine'.

e Some useful angles are explored here. This candidate would certainly be rewarded for the details given about operationalisation, number of items, etc. There is not the clarity that there was with the grade-A candidate, but the key details are given. As regards the way the data are processed, the candidate would benefit from a more systematic style of analysis. As it is, we are given some interesting findings, but are left wanting more detail. There is potential for a clear link with research aim 1, but it is not made.

Item 3 *'Have you ever felt that you were being encouraged to study a particular subject because of your sex?'*
The responses here were clear — none of my respondents could think of an occasion when they had had this experience.

Item 4 *'Have you ever felt that you were being discouraged from studying a particular subject?'*
The replies here were very different. One respondent said 'she [the French teacher] made it clear to us boys that girls were better at French than boys. After a time we just turned off — I'm not surprised most of my mates have not done French in the sixth form.'

This view was repeated by a number of boys, and not just for French. English teaching came in for the same criticism from a significant number of boys. For one subject or another, 50% of males said that they had experienced some sort of discrimination.

A female respondent summed up what a number of girls felt about (male) science teachers when she said, 'He was always really impatient with the girls when they did not get the point he was making straight away. But he was always spending more time with the boys, explaining things to them.' Approximately 30% of girls expressed some sort of view that they had not received equal treatment in science classes and that this had put them off some aspects of science.

e The candidate reports the findings from two items and provides some insight into classroom processes as perceived by pupils. Significant quotes and some quantitative data are given. An interesting set of observations is made, though the candidate neglects to point out that the majority of respondents did *not* report any experiences of discrimination.

Item 5 '*When you were in Year 11, what were the main factors that made you opt for the subjects you are now studying?*'
By far the most common reply here was 'career', though many respondents added that their ideas about their future job were still quite vague. This led to many of them saying that combined with the career angle was the fact that they had enjoyed the subject at GCSE. (Approximately 60% of respondents identified these two factors together.) Other reasons offered were that they liked the teachers involved (15%) and for subjects that are only studied in the sixth form, e.g. psychology, they said they were interested in the subject.

e This factual summary of the reasons offered by the respondents could have been elaborated further. If none of the respondents mentioned peer-group effect, this is an observation that the candidate ought to make. What you do not say is often as important as what you do say. Remember, you will score higher marks if you don't just analyse the data, but also make some interpretation points. This usually means going back to your aims.

Item 6 '*What effect did your family have on your choice of sixth form subjects?*'
My respondents were generally very definite about this. They stated very clearly that their parents had left it up to them to decide their final choice of subject. There was a 100% response for this view. So, in terms of subject choices and reasons for subject choices, these data would suggest that I need to look elsewhere for the reasons for choice, rather than in the family.

e When responding to the data from this item, the candidate tells the examiner exactly what the main message from the data is. The paragraph then goes on to say what the consequences are for the attempt to identify causal factors as regards gender and course choice, thus drawing meaning from the data gathered, not just describing the findings.

This grade-C candidate's Research section went on to ask questions about teacher expectations, peer pressure and career intention. The overall effect is good, with data being processed effectively, if only partially at times. The candidate needs to make more consistent and frequent links with the research question and aims in order to gain higher marks. There is evidence that some of the items on the questionnaire have drifted from the central focus of the research — you can see how they might generate valid data, but, equally, they might misfire. Item 6, on the family, could certainly have been worded in a more effective way — as it is, it is too general. The candidate did draw some final conclusions, but not strong ones, as the data did not support this. Overall, this is a reasonable section but in need of further development.

The Evaluation section

Grade-A candidate

Looking back over the research I have carried out I can now point out the strengths and weaknesses of the Personal Study.

- In terms of the basic research question and aims, I now feel that they were properly focused, clearly sociological and allowed me to research relevant aspects of gender and education.
- As far as my method is concerned, I am now confident that questionnaires were the most valid method as I outlined in my Rationale. They proved to be very efficient in terms of time and they ensured anonymity to people I knew personally, so their responses would be more honest, increasing validity. As everybody completed the same standardised questionnaire, the reliability should have been high too. However, I do feel that on some of the issues I tried to study, the method of interviewing would have allowed me to dig deeper and get more qualitative information from my respondents.
- As far as the data gathered are concerned, I feel they were also valid — they did describe aspects of course choice as I intended and this allowed me to conclude effectively. I do feel, though, that I have established correlations during the course of my research, rather than causal links. Nevertheless, some variables have been shown to be linked.
- My sample was obviously never going to rate highly as far as representativeness and generalisability go, but this was meant to be a piloting exercise, so a small sample was appropriate. I also built into the sample some aspects of randomness and a gender balance.

e From the start of this section, the examiner gets the clear impression that the candidate understands what evaluation is about and can give a balanced review of the research process. There is good use of the main methodological concepts, a degree of confidence about the method used, but also an acknowledgement that an alternative might have given more insight into some aspects of the topic. The sample is reconsidered along with other matters. Note too the candidate's concise, direct style of writing.

- My overall strategy worked well in terms of getting the questionnaires completed and returned. One possible flaw in my strategy was that I put psychology in the 'social science' subject group category. This is open to debate, as some might argue that it should go in the 'science' category, and this would have had a large impact on my findings. I didn't operationalise 'traditional masculine and feminine subjects' either and this is open to criticism too. In ethical terms, I ensured anonymity for my respondents and kept all data confidential.
- My questionnaire seemed to work well. When I trialled it, people commented that it was quite logical as regards the sequence of items and the number of items. In the actual survey it was effective. I was particularly happy with the way I worded Items 4 and 6, starting with quite neutral phrases which did not 'lead' the respondent to a highly personal response.

- As regards further development, it might be useful to combine student interviews with the existing questionnaires. This methodological pluralism would guarantee a breadth and depth of data which a single method would probably not. It might also be a good idea to interview teachers in schools with responsibility for equal opportunities. This would obviously add a new sample, but it would give another perspective on the gender and education debate.

This is a strong end to a high-quality study. The candidate finishes with three carefully thought-out observations and is not afraid to point out weaknesses in the strategy. This gains marks. The final two bullet points show an ability to look back and judge the effectiveness of certain aspects of the research exercise.

These extracts from the grade-A Personal Study should give you an indication of what to aim for. Remember, it does not have to be perfect to get grade A, but it does have to demonstrate all of the examinable skills at the highest level.

Grade-C candidate

My Personal Study was quite effective in many ways, though some things could have been done better. First of all, my method was valid. Questionnaires were the best way of gathering large amounts of information in a relatively quick way. The respondents were anonymous, so they would be more likely to be honest in their replies. My questionnaire was the result of a lot of careful thought and discussion with my teacher. I looked at questionnaires used by other sociologists, and used some of their ideas. The items produced the sort of data I needed to do my research. However, I feel that some of them did not produce detailed enough answers, which probably means that the wording of some items could have been better.

My sample had some representativeness built into it because I ensured both males and females were in it. However, it was a very small sample so you cannot generalise from it to the population at large. My general research strategy worked quite well. The questionnaires were given out efficiently and most of them were returned, completed properly.

If I were to develop the study further I would still use questionnaires, but I would triangulate by also doing interviews with a small group of careers advisers. This would give more qualitative data to add to the data from the questionnaires. A larger sample would also be a good idea so that representativeness could be built in better.

This final section has a number of satisfactory features but shows a tendency to be superficial. There is a set of evaluation angles that the candidate has obviously worked through, and many of the points made would gain marks. Some of the central methodological concepts (representativeness, validity, etc.) are included, although reliability is neglected, and the candidate also makes a comment about the quality of some of the questionnaire items. The comments about further development are satisfactory but not detailed enough. The candidate does not really explain the point of triangulation.

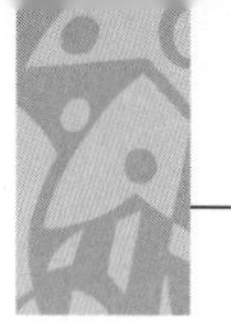

These extracts from the grade-C Personal Study reflect a piece of coursework with many strong points. However, if you compare it to the grade-A Personal Study extracts and refer to the Personal Study guidance section on pp. 12–18 of this guide, you will see the areas where improvements could have been made.